THE
WAY
TO
GAAMAAK
COVE

CIRQUE PRESS

Copyright © 2020 Doug Pope

Published by
Cirque Press

Sandra Kleven — Michael Burwell
3157 Bettles Bay Loop
Anchorage, AK 99515

cirquejournal@gmail.com
www.cirquejournal.com

Cover Photo by Doug Pope

Print ISBN 9798657125993

DEDICATION

To my best companion and critic, the beautiful Beth.

GAAMAAK

Gaamaak is a Chugachmiut Alutiiq word meaning "two rocks," but I didn't know that when Beth and I beached our kayaks in the light of a full moon along a spit jutting into Gaamaak Cove. Two towering rock faces, home for a large colony of nesting black-footed kittiwakes, had guided us since early evening down a long fjord known as Icy Bay. The spit was a natural landing spot after miles of rocky shores holding no refuge in high seas. Later, I imagined two qayaqs hauled up above the kelp line so Chugachmiut hunters could scout for seals resting on blocks of ice calving off Chenega Glacier. The hunters had come from the east on a long crossing, and the two rock faces signaled where the spit was long before it became a black line on the horizon. Had they come to gather kittiwake eggs as well? Alutiiq language has sounds English speakers are not familiar with, but each "aa" in Gaamaak is pronounced as we would pronounce the "a" in father. Two rocks, two kayaks, two humans, two faces red from the wind.

TABLE OF CONTENTS

KENNICOTT CROSSING

K etchikan, Alaska. November 1982. A commercial salmon troller rocked against the dock of Silver Lining Seafoods. It was a dreary day, spitting rain, wind blowing from the south up Tongass Narrows, and the dock timbers looked black, but the wooden boat was painted as white as white can be. I watched two men in full rain gear lift king salmon shimmering with iridescence out of the boat's hold. Friends Terry and Linda stood next to me in the office looking at a spreadsheet. Terry and I had been fellow bachelors in Southeast Alaska until he fell very much in love with Linda. I thought of a recent *Esquire* essay called "Pushing Forty," where the author got dumped by a younger woman and wondered if he'd blown his chances by being a bachelor too long. I turned away from the window and told Terry and Linda the woman they'd met in October, the woman I'd spent ten days with on a wilderness river, wasn't working out.

"She has a checklist, and she says we don't match up on paper all that well."

Linda turned and fixed her green eyes on mine. She was a skinny redhead with freckles and a becoming directness about her. After she and Terry fell in love, she'd come to visit me in Juneau. She had seen the climbing gear and kayak in my bedroom, and heard me joke I was just waiting to meet someone who still spoke to me after a week in a tent.

"Sounds like she knows what she wants. Have you thought about what's really important to you?"

I knew it was Linda's way of asking whether I was willing to make compromises. Had I been too rigid in my thinking? Did I have my own checklist too?

"I'm up for anything," I replied.

"I have a friend you might like to meet."

Linda told me Beth had worked for years on salmon boats but came ashore to work at Ketchikan Parks and Recreation after she'd become a mom.

"I've never dated a mom."

Linda smiled. Terry had been listening while looking at the spreadsheet. He'd grown up in Ketchikan and was one of those commercial fishermen others referred to as a "high liner." When I met him in Juneau, he was the youngest member of the Alaska legislature. His black hair was cut almost in a Beatles' style, and with his boyish grin he looked a little like Paul McCartney. Except for his black horn-rimmed glasses. He went on to become Speaker of the Alaska House of Representatives, and then left all that behind to found Silver Lining on the Ketchikan waterfront. I respected him as intelligent, thoughtful, and a clear thinker. He looked up from his figures.

"Beth's tall and smart and really built," he said.

What grabbed me when she first walked into Kay's Kitchen was the fur bomber jacket she wore with blue jeans. I pulled out a chair and helped her shrug off the jacket.

"Mink?" I asked.

She laughed out loud and pointed to a paint stain in the satin lining.

"It's muskrat. I found it in a dumpster."

I told her I was a lawyer but what I wanted to do was wilderness trips, and asked her about working on fishing boats. She said she loved spending summers on a gillnetter and always pined to explore the land beyond the shore, but when she became a mom, it meant her days at sea were numbered.

"As an infant, Natalie bounced in a jolly jumper hanging from the boom while I picked fish," she said. "Once she could walk, it didn't work to have her on deck."

Her prominent cheeks were still pink from a brisk November wind, and her teeth flashed when she smiled. Her long straight brown hair was parted in a way that made her oval face look like a gibbous moon, and I imagined her on deck of a fishing boat in rain gear with that smile. On the way out the door I asked if we could have lunch again the next day. She shook her head.

"I'm going to be in costume at a carnival for the kids."

The next morning I asked Linda where the carnival was being held and drove to the school. Inside a large room, all the parents were standing. From the back I spotted Beth. She was dressed in green tights that looked like they'd been painted on her long legs. A raven-haired girl in a white dress peaked around from behind her. When Beth saw me, her brow furrowed.

"What are you doing here?"

"I thought I'd sneak up on you. I'm sorry. Maybe I shouldn't have come."

She looked embarrassed, but introduced me to Natalie and said I could stick around. A month later she and I went to a hot tub party with Terry and Linda. After everyone else had dried off and gone back in the house, I stuck my face underwater to kiss her breasts. She grabbed a towel and jumped over the side.

"I have to go," she said.

I learned she was trying to get rid of an on-again off-again boyfriend and started checking in whenever I was in Ketchikan. At a dalliance one night in my room in an old hotel, I told her I was going to hold back until he was out of the picture. In the spring, I called her to see how she was doing. She told me she'd gotten rid of the boyfriend, and that Natalie was going to be with her father in August. I started talking about the Wrangell Mountains in eastern Alaska, where I had spent a lot of time in the seventies.

"It's a Grand Canyon like scene with limestone and sandstone walls, but there are also snow and ice capped mountains rising behind the rims."

I said there was an historic trail leading up the Chitistone River through Chitistone Canyon, and then on into Canada.

"The trail's been there since the gold rush and there's a landing strip near the entrance. Let's do it."

"What about before then?" she asked.

I answered I'd be there in July. But July didn't go well. I was over-committed between Silver Lining and my law practice, and ended up leaving Ketchikan early. Beth didn't hide her disappointment.

"You must have known," she said.

Then it was August, we were in my Juneau house preparing for the trip, and hadn't seen each other since early July. I thought of myself as a real outdoorsman, prepared for anything, and had already packed my custom-made expedition backpack with sleeping bag, rain gear, stove, and cookware. It sat on a bench in my bedroom where I stood hovering while Beth sat on her heels and pulled items from her backpack. I'd asked to see her clothes and gear, but I felt claustrophobic when she spread them out.

Too much stuff.

"The Chitistone Canyon is no weenie roast," I said.

It was something only a jerk would say. I knew it as soon as it came out of my mouth. But, I didn't take it back. Right then, I was looking for an easy way out, and a card laid is a card played a guy once told me. When Beth finished packing and looked up, her brown eyes blazed with questions, and I thought I had mousetrapped myself by my big talk. That evening we went to dinner at a dockside restaurant. Beth's face flushed with excitement when I answered her questions about the Wrangell Mountains. I decided to relax into the idea.

We are going to Chitistone Canyon.

Three days later we stood at the end of a long gravel road from the old railroad town Chitina, staring at the main channel of the Kennicott River. A cable stretched six hundred feet across it, and next to the cable was a hand-painted sign that read "TRAM." The tram consisted of wooden planks hanging from two pulleys riding on top the cable. The idea, we figured out, was for us to sling a leg over the planks, get centered, reach overhead, and pull on the cable. From the end of the road it was our only way into McCarthy, an historic mining town where we hoped to find someone with a small plane.

With Beth behind me we straddled the wooden planks, tied on our backpacks, and reached overhead. The cable sagged low over a charcoal colored train of breaking waves in the middle of the river. At first, we only inched out toward the water's edge over a rocky bar twenty feet below us. As the sag in the cable steepened, we picked up speed. In a heartbeat we were pitched downhill toward the rapids. I felt a bump behind me and heard Beth gasp. The tram bottomed out and slowed to a stop, our feet dangling above near black waves crashing like cymbals. A steep gravel bank on the far side looked like the grey walls of a castle. We reached up and pulled on the cable, then grabbed it again before the tram could backslide.

Pull and grab. Pull and grab. Pull and grab. Pull and grab. Pull and grab.

We were breathing hard and sweaty when we reached the top of the far bank, tied off the tram, and started walking toward a second channel. Beth was quiet and her jaw seemed twisted. She looked down at her right hand. Her blue Patagonia glove was torn and blood oozed out.

"My glove got caught in the pulley."

Afraid to pull the glove off there on a dusty trail, I thought of a mossy spot where I used to dip for water.

"There is a spring ahead."

She nodded and we kept going: away from the main channel along an old railroad bed, across a smaller channel on a second tram, over a wooden footbridge and down a path bordered by willows and alder, until we knelt at the edge of a shallow spring spilling out from moss covered rocks. The air was dank and the light was fading fast. Beth pulled off her glove.

Bone gleamed from a deep gash along the length of her index finger.

Blue fibers stuck out of the wound. She looked into my eyes. I dipped my bandanna into the spring and wiped her brow and neck. I put my mouth to her ear and whispered I was going to start closing the wound. She grimaced while I used the tweezers of my Swiss Army knife to pull out the fibers, one by one, and looked away when I closed the gash with butterflies, starting at the narrow end. She waited patiently while I carved a willow into a splint with my knife and taped it in place. Rain started falling. I looked down at our reflection in the pool, and thought I saw a hooded ghost.

"I'm tired," she said.

We searched in the dark for the McCarthy Lodge. Yellow light from kerosene lamps led along a boardwalk to a screen door. I pushed through into a small room with a sign on the wall that said to leave all weapons at the door. A mustachioed bartender with an apron told me in a quiet voice the lodge was full, but he led us outside and waved his flashlight across the dirt street toward an abandoned two-story building. I held Beth by the arm while we climbed a narrow wooden stairway to the second floor and walked down a hallway. We peered into each room with our headlamps. At the end was a room with a window overlooking the lodge. Stained cotton curtains hung down weathered wooden trim. Metal springs perched on an iron bed frame. I inflated our sleeping pads, laid them on top, and coaxed Beth into her sleeping bag.

She slept on and off for the next two days while I brought bowls of oatmeal and mushroom soup from the lodge. When she was awake, she talked about the fog of loss she felt when her older sister and dad were killed in a car accident. I told her about growing up outside Fairbanks, and escaping with a friend to Anchorage in a 1954 Mercury the night we graduated from high school. On the third day she stuck her nose under an armpit and asked how she could get clean. I pulled aside a cotton curtain and pointed toward the lodge.

"There's an outdoor shower," I said.

It had plywood sides, a blue tarp for a door, and a dirt floor. Beth held her splinted finger in the air while I washed her back and front with a soapy bandanna, all the way down her long legs. She bent over and I washed her hair, pouring water from a battered aluminum pitcher while working in suds with one hand. On a rocky path back to the abandoned hotel, I stopped and said we could backtrack across the tram and drive a hundred miles to Glenallen where there was a clinic.

"We'd only lose a couple of days," I said.

She frowned.

"We just got here. I don't want to go back."

Gutsy woman.

We found a local pilot named Jim Edwards, a thin man in his sixties with a shy smile who had spent his adult life in the Wrangell Mountains. He took to Beth right away, and invited us to dinner at his log house at the end of a grass airstrip for his Piper airplane.

Sun glinted off contorted limestone walls of the Mile High Cliffs when Jim banked right. We crossed a broad floodplain and started up the Chitistone River, flying under a ceiling of weather stacked up against steep mountains. Waterfalls fell out of clouds and bounced over narrow ledges down grey rock faces streaked with brown. One had gouged out a hotel-sized room, and grey clouds reflected in a pool perched on the edge of the rock in front of the waterfall. I imagined being there with Beth on a sunny after-noon, kicking across the pool on our backs, staring up at a cathedral roof, and crawling out to peer over the lip down the vertical face to a muddy river flashing with whitewater. By the time we touched down on a gravel landing strip, raindrops hit the windshield. Jim kept the plane pointed into the wind while we unloaded our packs. He looked at Beth and waved toward a line of spruce on the far side of a brushy gravel bar.

"A trapper's cabin is over there."

Beyond "over there" was a trail along the Chitistone River leading into the canyon. We shouldered our packs and leaned into the wind. I won-dered where Beth and I were headed.

RIVER
OF BEARS

My roommate Mitch and I were opposites in many ways. He often strode about the streets of downtown Juneau in a custom bolero jacket, silk scarf, and red ostrich skin boots. I just as often would be wearing blue river shorts, a Grateful Dead t-shirt, and running shoes. Our taste in women differed too. Whenever I heard leather boots tapping up the boardwalk to our house, I knew it was a fashionably dressed woman in a wool coat coming to see Mitch. Any woman who came to see me wore rain gear and rubber boots.

On a warm Sunday in late July, Mitch stretched out on our couch reading a copy of the *New York Times*, while I sat at a table studying maps of a remote river in Western Alaska.

"Beth's coming in three days."

Mitch sat up. He and Beth had met once. A broad smile pushed through his beard. I nodded.

"She'll be here for most of a week."

"What's this, playing house?"

"We're getting ready for a river trip."

He shrugged with his hands out and palms upturned.

"Long distance romances, you gotta' love'em."

Before I met Beth, I had been dumped by a couple of women and I wondered if I even understood them. Once, when we were standing in the kitchen of her small house beside Ketchikan Creek, I said if a woman told me she was seeking a sensitive man, I thought what she was really looking for was a bad boy. Beth put her arms around me, got her moon shaped face close to mine, and looked at me with half a smile.

"What we need is more of this and less of that," she said.

Still, I was ambivalent, and thought the distance between Juneau and Ketchikan was like a border. Beth called me that winter when two women friends of Mitch were visiting him at our house.

"Can we talk?" she asked.

"Now's not good."

"When?"

"Beth, I have a life."

She said "goodbye" in a quiet voice and hung up. I thought about it for a couple of weeks and then called to say I'd be in Ketchikan for two days to work at Silver Lining.

"Let's have dinner at The Fireside," I said.

Beth agreed. After I arrived, I realized I was way overcommitted and called again.

"It's going to have to be lunch."

"What happened?"

"Things are more complicated than I anticipated."

The next day I fidgeted in front of her.

"Something's come up. I only have time for takeout."

We walked to a food stand on the wharf that served halibut tacos. The day was grey and the air smelled of grease and diesel exhaust. She turned, took both my hands in hers, and looked right at me with her dark brown eyes.

"I'm letting you off the hook."

"What?"

"I'm letting you off the hook. You don't have any obligation to me."

"What if I don't want to be let off the hook?"

She was quiet while a pickup lumbered by.

"Don't you?"

I stood there silently, looking at the ground, grasping for words, while Beth explained she was fine with us just being friends.

"I don't want to be just friends," I said.

So, we kept up the dance. In the spring, Beth told me Natalie was going to spend August again with her father. I started talking up the Andreafsky River in Western Alaska. It drains south out of the Nulato Hills, a vast billowing sea of tundra and taiga separating the flats of the middle Yukon River from the Bering Sea coast. Before it empties into the Yukon near the Yup'ik village of St. Mary's, the Andreafsky meanders for many miles through lowlands, around lakes, and between hills with spruce and birch forests part way up their flanks. I told Beth I had flown up it once in a small plane on the way to Unalakleet, an Inupiaq town on the Norton Sound coast.

"The water was so clear we could see salmon crowding into pools from hundreds of feet up. We didn't see one cabin or even a boat."

"Show me," Beth asked.

We looked at a big map of Alaska pinned on a hallway wall. I put my finger on Unalakleet, and drew south through the Nulato Hills to the northern end of a squiggly blue line, forty miles from the coast.

"It's over a hundred and twenty miles from the headwaters to the Yukon at St. Mary's. I doubt we'll see anyone else down its whole length."

"I'd really like to do it," Beth said.

I started looking for information. My well-worn guidebook, *Wild Rivers of Alaska*, by a guy who had travelled all over with his wife in collapsible Klepper kayaks, made no mention of the Andreafsky. I went to the State library, but the only thing I could find was a government report recommending it be designated a National Wild and Scenic River. At one place the report referred to the Andreafsky as a "river of bears." That was okay with me. I was confident I knew bears. I'd camped in bear country, seen blond tundra grizzlies and coastal brown bears, and even chased a skinny blond one off once with a firecracker when I saw it lumbering downriver. I knew people carried twelve-gauge shotguns with rifled slugs, but I'd never carried a defensive weapon in the outdoors. I had hunted ducks and geese with a pump twenty-gauge since I was a kid, so I decided to carry one with both rifled slugs and birdshot. I thought there was a chance we might shoot a duck or a ptarmigan for food. I explained all this to my friend Bob, who had flown all over bush Alaska in his plane. Bob carried a .300 Weatherby rifle.

"Twenty-gauge," he snorted, "that's real bear country out there."

I reminded him of the time we fished the Stuyahok River for rainbow trout in Western Alaska, and what a pain it was to carry the Weatherby.

"Maybe so," he growled, "but it will knock a bear on its ass."

He said I was a fool to be out there with anything less than a twelve-gauge and slugs. I guess I was just loyal to the shotgun I knew. I rationalized that the muzzle velocity was nearly the same.

It's just that the slug is smaller.

In an Anchorage paper, Hermann's Air advertised a $99 special from Anchorage to St. Mary's. I called Stan Hermann in St. Mary's and told him we wanted to float the main fork of the Andreafsky.

"No one's been up there in years," he said.

I asked if he had a Super Cub, the quintessential two-place bush plane capable of carrying big loads and landing almost anywhere.

"Yup."

"Can you drop us off at the headwaters?"

"It'll take two trips."

When I told Mitch that Beth and I were going to spend a few days preparing for a river trip, he said he needed to go to Seattle anyway to look at furniture for his waterfront antique store. He left the same morning Beth flew up from Ketchikan. It'd been three months since we'd seen each other. She'd gotten a permanent, and her brown hair, which had been straight and framed her face like a gibbous moon, was wavy and bouncy. Instead of looking like crew on a salmon boat, she looked more like a professional woman. I wondered what I had gotten myself into.

I didn't own a car in those days, and we caught a cab to downtown Juneau. I made small talk on the way but Beth just nodded and was quiet. I wondered if the whole river trip thing was a good idea. At my house, we stood looking at wooden pieces of my Klepper kayak that showed a lot of wear from previous trips. I began talking about how the Andreafsky was really remote, picked up a kayak piece, and pointed it at her.

"It is real bear country out there. Do we really know each other well enough for this kind of trip?"

She took one step and stood right in front of me, her face inches from mine, eyebrows arched, brown eyes flashing.

"Doug Pope. You promised me a trip down the Andreafsky River. You're not backing out of it now."

I looked down. She took the kayak piece out of my hand.

"What I do see is the bright work on these ash pieces is where I can help."

Over the next four days, Beth sanded and varnished each of eighteen Klepper pieces, some as long as three feet, using materials she purchased at a downtown hardware store. After the varnish dried, she sanded each piece again with finer grit and put on a second coat. I focused on repairing holes in the Klepper's synthetic rubber hull and working on food and camping gear, including sewing a sling for the twenty-gauge. We had pleasant meals and slept in the same bed, but our conversations focused on logistics. The line I had drawn felt like a canyon.

When we arrived in Anchorage on a jet from Juneau, we were dressed for the river in synthetic tops and bottoms, red XTRATUF boots, and bright bandannas tied around our necks. I picked up the morning paper on the way to the counter for Hermann's Air, but didn't open it until we were in a small twin-engine plane on the way to St. Mary's. On the front page was a story about a brown bear attacking the first guy in a line of fishermen walking through an alder thicket near Lake Iliamna. The bear had the first guy's head in its jaws when the third guy, who was carrying a twelve-gauge with slugs, finally got to the scene. He shot the bear three times. Each blast knocked the bear backwards over a bank. Each time it got back on its feet and came back up the bank. It took the fourth shot to put it down for good. The guy whose head was in the bear's mouth lived but one eyeball had popped out. I handed the paper to Beth. She read the story without saying a word.

In St. Mary's, Stan Hermann stood in front of a hangar checking the gas in his white Super Cub with red wings. Stan was a short guy with a mustache and wore a navy blue cap with a white bow above the bill. The Super Cub was a classic Alaska bush plane, with modified wings and wide dragster slicks on reversed chrome wheels for landing on tundra and gravel bars. Stan had a brusque manner about him. He shook his head when he saw the two canvas Klepper bags. He pulled the long parts out and stacked them on the floor behind the pilot's seat. He told me to get in the back seat with my feet on top and stuffed gear and food bags around my legs and on my knees. He climbed in the pilot's seat, handed me a pair of earplugs, and cranked the engine. I gave thumbs up to Beth when we taxied out onto the paved airport. As soon as the Cub lifted off, Stan banked over the mile wide Yukon, over log cabins on a bluff above the mouth of the Andreafsky, and headed upriver.

After nearly an hour, we passed over timberline. Patches of alder and willow lined the river's edge, but everything else was green tundra so vibrant it seemed to glow. I reached over Stan's shoulder to point out a blond grizzly on a gravel bar. He looked but said nothing. Then, I pointed at a light brown one feeding in a berry patch. He didn't even look. On a bend in the river between tundra-covered hills, he circled a short gravel bar. A brown grizzly with a blond stripe down its back dug for something at the downriver end. Stan circled one more time and buzzed the grizzly. It reared up on its hind legs, waved its paws at the dragster slicks as we flew just overhead, dropped down on all fours, and ran toward a line of brush. We came in low and touched down, wings rocking up and down while the Cub bounced down the bar. I jumped out and started unloading while Stan kept the engine running.

"Which way did it go?"

He shrugged, closed the door, and pushed the throttle. Dust blew up as the Cub careened down the bar until it lifted off at the water's edge and climbed steeply. While Stan banked into a long circle and flew overhead, I pulled the twenty-gauge out of the gear, shoved four rifled slugs into the magazine, and slung it over my shoulder. The river was shallow with banks guarded by scrub birch and willows their own shade of green. When I splashed across it in my rubber boots, a brown speckled curlew with a long curved beak flushed along the opposite bank. Islands of yellow arctic poppies surrounded a mound of verdant tundra, and I walked up it to get a better view. On hillsides all around, green jointed grasses and edgy sedges psychedelically swayed in a voiceless breeze. I stood very still, straining to hear any sound, any rustle, but all I could hear was the whisper of running water.

Two hours later, Stan was back. He flew low upriver, banked the Cub into a wide arc, and landed down river again. He turned around at the water's edge and taxied toward me. Beth stepped out and we unloaded the rest of the gear and food while Stan kept the engine running.

"Did you see those bears?" she asked.

She told me she spotted a sow and two cubs on the final approach.

"And there's a blond grizzly just downriver."

Stan waved and pushed the throttle again. The Cub lifted off just before the bar ended and sailed downriver with the dragster slicks inches above the riffles. My mind started racing ahead. I unslung the shotgun, pumped a round into the chamber, and checked the safety.

"We may want to move our camp in the morning," I said.

"Do you really think that's a problem?"

"I don't think we should stay around long enough for them to figure out we're here."

We assembled the Klepper and repacked the gear, but that night a coastal storm moved in off the Bering Sea. In the morning, wind gusted upriver and we could see our breath. We pulled on full rain gear and climbed up a green-gold slope to a spot where we could see the river winding out of sight. The light was poor, like dusk in the middle of the day, but we could see a grizzly splashing hundreds of yards downriver. Beth pointed out a dark mass below it.

"Isn't that another one?"

I felt a shiver and turned back toward camp. The storm was in full swing, so we stayed the night. Early the next morning, I showed Beth a handheld foghorn and pushed a button. It shrieked like a dying animal and echoed off the hills.

"We should use it before we go around a blind corner. We may not have time to beach the kayak if one is in the river."

"That means we're not going to see any bears."

We climbed in the kayak. I nestled the shotgun between my legs, and set the foghorn on top of the spray cover where I could reach it with the paddle in my hands. Once around the first bend, the river turned narrow and fast. When we came to tight bends, I pushed the button and the foghorn shrieked. Sure enough, we didn't see any bears. In mid-afternoon the kayak went aground in a riffle, and a sharp piece of shale sliced a four-inch gash in the hull. Water poured in while we hopped out and grabbed the lines. The kayak floated free but was heavy, and food and gear bags floated inside. We dragged it to a rocky beach where I reached in and handed out stuff sacks to Beth while she took them to higher ground. We each grabbed an end and rolled the kayak over. I covered it with a tarp and lit our camp stove under it to heat the space. In an hour the hull was dry enough to patch with duct tape, but it was late so we camped facing the channel, food bags stashed under a tarp fifty yards downriver in line of sight from our tent door.

The temperature dropped again and black clouds rushed upriver as darkness lay upon us. Heavy rain pounded the fly of our dome tent. In the middle of the night, Beth shook me awake.

"Can you hear that?"

Water splashed behind our tent. The channel we had dragged out of was in front.

"THE FOOD BAGS," she cried.

I unzipped the tent door and shined the beam of my headlamp out into the night. Sheets of rain, like dark scrims, concealed the cache. I got out of the tent, took a few steps, and saw that a new channel behind us was already running six inches deep. Our rocky beach had turned into an island. I stumbled my way to the cache, moved the food bags to the highest spot I could find, and used flat slate stones to hold down the tarp. When Beth unzipped the door, I dove through. She shivered. I put my arm over her while we listened to the storm slam into the tent.

The next morning brought a warm sun. We spread out gear to dry on top of the kayak and lingered. The green hills had scattered spruce trees and lush tundra, so when the kayak was packed, we paddled across the river to climb one. A fresh track of a tundra grizzly pressed deep in the mud where we beached. It reminded me of a confectioner's work on a fancy cake with chocolate curling away from the edges. I spread out both hands inside. It was the biggest bear track I'd ever seen. We lingered on the hillside where the tundra was like a wet sponge, and lay side-by-side in our rain gear on a thick carpet of white reindeer moss speckled with red, looking at the sky. An hour later, we buttoned up the spray cover of the kayak, shoved off, and drifted in the sun. The twenty-gauge lay between my legs. The river slowly coursed through a series of shallow pools. It was hardly necessary to dip a paddle, the sun was warm on my face, and I felt relaxed.

At last, at last, this is what we came for.

Around a corner, a large dark brown grizzly stepped out of willows on a high gravel bank and stood on its haunches. Beth had her head down, fiddling with her camera.

"Bear," I whispered.

We both turned while the kayak drifted. The grizzly charged straight at us down the gravel bank with ears pinned back. I fumbled with unbuttoning the spray skirt while trying to reach for the shotgun. The grizzly galloped across a riverside pool like a horse splashing across a river, with water spraying high off both shoulders. I thought it looked like a torpedo coming straight at us; its forehead just kept getting bigger and bigger while its legs were a blur. I pumped a round into the shotgun's chamber and pushed hard on the rudder to swing the bow out of the way. I didn't really aim, just pointed the muzzle above the charging grizzly's head. When I pulled the trigger, it kept coming. I realized then the twenty-gauge really was a popgun, and a vision flashed through my mind of the grizzly on its hind legs in the middle of the river, claws waving, and me vaulting out of the kayak and shoving the shotgun's muzzle in its gaping mouth.

And then. Then. How many heartbeats were there? The grizzly wheeled, plunged into the deep part of the channel, and swam for the opposite bank. A loud hiss came from behind us while it climbed out. I turned in my seat. A brown cub with ears alert peered out through some willows. The sow and cub scampered toward each other along a grassy bank and stood side-by-side, hissing as we drifted past. My throat was dry and my hand shook when I reached for a water bottle. Beth smiled and held up her camera. She'd gotten photos.

Downstream, spawning pink salmon crowded pools and slithered up shallow riffles. Grizzlies had trampled wide trails in the grass on both sides of the river and littered them with mutilated carcasses. I pointed to one trail nearly as wide as the street in front of Beth's Ketchikan house.

"You could drive your Rambler down that."

We started seeing flocks of noisy waterfowl crowding gravel bars: Canada geese, white-fronted geese, trumpeter swans, tundra swans, all molting and unable to fly. That night we camped on a long gravel bar winding around the base of a low hill. Molting adult geese and swans and their young swarmed the upper end, concentrating in gravel patches without any brush. On the lower end, willows shielded a marsh from view. The air was thick with the stench of rotting fish. While Beth walked down to check the marshy area out, I pitched our tent on a bare spot right along the water's edge where we wouldn't disturb the birds. Beth came back with her brow wrinkled.

"It looks pretty beary down there."

The sky turned dark and we settled into the tent. In the middle of the night geese began chirping and barking and honking. Swans started trumpeting and bugling. They kept at it, with more birds adding their voices to the ensemble until a cacophony of chirping and barking and honking and trumpeting and bugling moved around our tent into the river and drifted away. The entire waterfowl population of the gravel bar had vacated in total darkness.

It has to be a bear.

I gripped the cold steel of the shotgun, fondled the trigger guard, and listened for every sound. When a breeze rustled the willows, I bolted upright, index finger on the trigger, thumb on the safety, straining to hear any signal of movement. After a long silence, I lay back down and dozed off. Then it happened again. In the morning, while the tent warmed from the sun's first rays, Beth sat up and stretched her arms.

"I never had such a good sleep."

We saw grizzlies up close for several days, fishing in the river, splashing down side streams, moving along cut banks above the gravel bars. I thought more bears must be in the brush away from the river's edge, sleeping off the feasting binge from the salmon run.

There must be ten for each one we've seen.

Beth thought it was pretty cool.

"It's so exhilarating to be reminded every day we aren't the dominant species," she said.

I had talked big about seeking out rivers where there weren't any footprints, where it was truly wild. When I got what I really asked for, I was on edge during the day and slept in fits and starts. One evening, on a long narrow gravel bar, Beth relaxed in the tent after we finished a meal of pasta and smoked salmon. A gentle breeze blew across the bar, carrying our scent into willows along a cut bank. A dark shape moved behind them and I heard a loud snort. I leaned over by the tent door.

"Did you hear that?"

My throat was dry and my voice squeaked. No answer. I looked through the bug screen. Beth was reading a book.

"Bear," I said in a loud voice.

She didn't look up.

"They seem to be giving us a wide berth."

I wandered out on the bar, grabbed some driftwood, and came back to start a fire so smoke would drift toward the willows. Beth stuck her head out.

"Don't you want to come in?"

"I think I'll stay up and stoke the fire for awhile."

Color faded in the sky above the western hills while I dragged the biggest root systems I could handle and threw them on the fire until yellow flames swayed above my head. Light from the fire flickered on the willows along the cut bank, and I scanned them again and again for any reflection from a bear's eyes. When the fire at last turned into orange coals with grey along the edges, I crawled into the tent and dozed off and on until the sun rose.

We started seeing bigger salmon in the pools and stopped where the river braided into two channels. Beth's pole bent double on the first cast. She horsed one ashore, a bright chum salmon Yukon River people call "silvers," and started filleting it on the blade of her kayak paddle.

"We can use two," she said.

I walked upriver around an alder thicket and heard splashing ahead in a side stream covered by a willow arbor. A blondish grizzly stepped into the sun and looked my direction. I pointed the shotgun in the air and pulled the trigger. The bear spun around on its hind legs and splashed back up under the arbor. But, the splashing didn't stop, so I fired off another round. Beth walked around the alder thicket.

"What's the matter?"

"Think of it as a noisemaker."

"They're not being aggressive. Can't you stop shooting?"

I made a show of ejecting the rest of the slugs out on the ground in front of her. When she rolled her eyes and walked away, I slipped them into my day bag. We camped that night on a long gravel bar with a panoramic

view across a broad tundra valley to a band of forested hills. Another storm
came in, and the bar with a panoramic view turned into an exposed spot. It
was still blowing the next day, so we ended up staying another night. Soon after we shoved off, the river entered a dense spruce forest, and we stopped seeing blond grizzlies or blondish grizzlies or brown grizzlies with blond stripes.

On a beach below a low gravel bluff, Beth cast into a deep pool. Red
flashed in the bottom. She'd hooked into a large arctic char. I climbed up a
bank to get a view downriver. Deep, pigeon-toed depressions peregrinated
across a lush meadow along the top of the bluff. I tiptoed in them over a little
rise, twisting my ankles like I was back dancing the mash in high school. Just
downriver, hidden from Beth's view by an overhanging alder bush, two dark
chocolate brown bears stood waist deep in the middle of the current, waiting
for salmon swimming upriver. They had their backs to me and the afternoon
breeze blew upriver to my advantage. I turned toward Beth, wanting her
to see them, wanting her to decide, but the pigeon toed-trail stopped me. I
turned again. The brown bears were just out of my line of sight. My mind
whirled. I thought of Harrison Ford in *Raiders of the Lost Ark.*

Why did it have to be more bears?

I held up the foghorn. It shrieked. When we shoved off, a red-bellied
char lay on the bottom of the kayak. The brown bears were nowhere to be
seen. Beth turned to look back at me, her face wrinkled with emotion.

"I never got to see them."

Those were the last bears we encountered. A day later we entered
the lower river, where spruce trees leaned over the current, and beavers had
dropped big cottonwoods along the banks. The sun was hot and the blue
canvas deck of the kayak felt warm. Beth stripped down to a t-shirt, and we
stroked in cadence while I whistled the tune to "Wings of a Dove." In late afternoon, shadows grew long across the river and the temperature fell off fast.
Beth's paddling became erratic. I noticed her shoulders seemed to be twisted.
She set her paddle down and looked back over her shoulder.

"I'm just real sleepy."

I drew the kayak toward a narrow gravel beach and helped her out. I started putting up the tent and asked her to pull out the stove. She dropped it twice.

"You're hypothermic," I said.

"It's too early to camp," she protested.

I put an arm around her and led her through the tent door to the sleeping bags I'd zipped together. She lay on her side with her face down when I covered her.

"Hold me," she said.

I wrapped my arms around her, and buried my nose in the nape of her neck to savor the smell of her body while the current sighed by. Two days later, when we beached the kayak at a muddy boat landing, puffy white clouds reflected in water as broad and placid as a lake. We'd arrived at St. Mary's. That night we lay naked on a plank floor by a barrel stove glowing orange in a friend's weathered log cabin. After so many days in a tent, it felt like we were in a sauna, and drops of sweat on Beth's shoulder and neck tasted sweet. I thought of her sagacious mind and perfect breasts. In the morning, I walked down a muddy street to the village store, a low building covered with corrugated metal roofing. The phone hung on a wall by a bulletin board with handwritten cards listing things for sale. Each said to call on a CB frequency. I called Mitch.

"Wilderness boy. Did you and Beth survive the week in a tent?"

"We did."

That evening, when the sun was low, we walked to the top of a hill behind rows of greying log cabins. We looped our arms around each other's waists and looked north. Green tundra rolled like an ocean swell toward the Nulato Hills, ablaze in gold from the setting sun.

VIENTO BLANCO

Mitch and I stared at empty glasses on the bar of the Alaska Hotel. Ronald Reagan had just been re-elected president. When three guys in business suits ordered Crown Royal and water, Mitch tossed a five on the bar and we started home in a cold rain. On the way up wooden steps, I looked over my shoulder.

"Beth's moving here."

Water dripped from his beard.

"Do I need to find another place?"

"She's renting an apartment. "

"Weren't you going on a mountain trip?"

"I haven't broken it to her yet."

When Beth returned from the Andreafsky and learned Natalie was going to spend the fourth grade in Bellingham, she put her house in Ketchikan up for sale and announced she was moving to Juneau. She said it was time to find out if our relationship had a future. I thought it was a gutsy move, but it made me really nervous. The night she drove her Rambler station wagon off the ferry, I told her I was leaving for South America with Dave and Terry. She blinked but didn't complain. She knew both of them. Dave had charmed her in the spring with his sunny demeanor after he and I had spent ten days climbing in the Ruth Gorge near Denali. She liked it when I said he was fearless and pushed us to do things I hadn't imagined, but I kept us from killing ourselves. Terry's girlfriend Linda was one of Beth's best friends, and she knew him as a strong and energetic outdoorsman. I promised I'd only be gone a month.

For weeks, Dave and I had been talking about where to spend January climbing in the southern hemisphere. From the beginning, I said we should go to Aconcagua in western Argentina, the tallest mountain in South America. I imagined being at a party when someone nodded my direction and said quietly, "He's been on the top of the highest mountains in North and South America." In the end, Dave said he could agree as long as we did the more remote "Polish Route," named for the first ascent team in 1934. It was accessible by a horse trail off a two-lane highway in a mountain pass to Chile. In the middle of the pass on the Argentine side sits Puente del Inca, once the southernmost outpost of the Incas, where rock dwellings still cling to canyon walls along the Rio Las Cuevas.

An outfitter named Fernando Grajales based his operation there out of a storage shed attached to a lodge with peeling red paint. He smoked a hand-rolled cigarette while saying he could arrange for two gauchos with horses and mules to haul our gear to basecamp for the Polish Route. We left our passports and wallets in Fernando's heavy iron safe and he hauled us in the back of his rusty pickup to the trailhead, where we met Ramón and Ecedrio, each with coal black hair and dressed in blue jeans with dusty hats and cotton bandannas. They strapped our duffels onto two mules, mounted horses, and set out on a trail through a desert valley up the Rio Vacas. We scrambled to keep up and took shelter under our bandannas from a brutal sun. Thorns grabbed at our synthetic gear and every plant seemed to have spines. When the sun disappeared behind the mountains and the temperature dropped, we crossed the Rio Vacas to spend the night at a refugio with one rock wall collapsed and the roof caved in. Ecedrio gathered mesquite from a hillside and Ramón built a fire. They finished their roasted slabs of beef and toasted hard rolls before water boiled on our kerosene stove. While we mixed hot water into freeze-dried packets, they crawled under a piece of corrugated metal roofing to sleep.

In the morning, we started up a trail along a creek cascading down a gorge. Climbers descended, passing us in various states of disarray. Their message was the same. It was cold up high and they were escaping it.

"Negative 30," one said.

He disappeared down the trail before I could ask if he was talking Centigrade or Fahrenheit. Another, with frostbitten feet wrapped in dirty cotton bandages, shouted from the back of a black mule.

"A FROZEN BODY IS STILL UP THERE."

The trail crossed brushy cornrows of moraine to the basecamp, called Plaza Argentina, just below where the Relinchos Glacier squeezed out between rocky spires and a canyon wall. The Aconcagua pyramid dominated in the distance, with the Polish Glacier twisting down the East Face. There weren't any ranger stations, platforms, cook shacks, or privies then. Just three clusters of brightly colored tents scattered hundreds of yards apart. We were at 12,000 feet, and it was the last stop for the gauchos. Ahead were long fields of nieves penitentes, skinny pyramids of ice, some twelve feet tall, clustered in formations so tight you had to squeeze between them. Beyond, an even steeper trail switched back and forth across talus slopes until it disappeared. A waxing gibbous moon floated above rock bands on the right side of the face.

We took our time acclimating, moving food and fuel and climbing gear higher during long days, descending into thicker air in the evening for sleep. The altitude affected each of us in different ways. Terry sat down once in plummeting temperatures and needed help pulling out his down coat. I caught up with Dave at a ledge where he'd fallen asleep on his backpack in the sun. A nagging cough reminded me of difficult times above 16,000 on Denali. Two other American teams moved ahead of us and disappeared.

We settled into our own rhythms of carrying and resting. During hours on the trail, where a long shadow was my only companion, I debated giving up bachelorhood. There was so much I admired about Beth. But, was I really ready to settle down?

The trail steepened and the weather deteriorated as the days went on. On the lip of a giant cirque at 16,000 we encountered our first blizzard. It was my night to cook, and I decided to make smoked salmon fettuccine. I sat on my heels outside the tent door while reaching inside to toss the salmon, pasta, and grated cheese in a pan Terry held over the flame from the stove. The blowing snow was wet and heavy and clung to my back and neck while water dripped off my nose. In the morning the sun shone again. Two condors circled above us and then landed close by, no doubt watching for any unprotected food bags. A few days later, the second blizzard swept in after we had established a camp next to a rock tower at 18,000 where the Polish Glacier played out beneath the East Face. When Terry and I dropped down a long talus slope headed for a cache of supplies, it was calm. On the way back a ferocious wind blew in. Within minutes we were in a whiteout of snow as fine as sifted flour. Local climbers had warned that "viento blanco" could damage lungs, so we wrapped scarves around our heads to cover our faces, and I led us up by orienting off lurking shadows of towering rock buttresses.

At the camp, high winds rocketed in from the Atlantic system and fine snow clung to the downwind side of the tent. Terry and I leaned against the aluminum poles while Dave fiddled with our stove we couldn't seem to keep running at that altitude. We could hear the gusts coming. First it was a low-pitched moan from the downslope direction of two rocky towers, building to a loud howl before the gust hammered the side of the tent. There was always a lull. Just enough to get us hopeful, but then we'd hear the moan again.

After one lull, the winds pivoted and gusts pounded us from a different direction. The poles on the far side of our dome tent started to collapse. I leaped like a frog across our sleeping bags, grabbed a pole, and shouldered it away from being pinned to the ground. A moment later an outburst of wind drove straight down like an incoming comet. The tent bulged out on all sides and Terry jumped into the middle with his back bent and straightened his legs to push up. At morning twilight, the gusts stopped and we couldn't hear any incoming. I unzipped the tent door and peaked out. Waves of wind packed snow rippled across rocky slopes.

Dave and I glassed the face for a safe line. A series of serrated rock bands loomed above us on the right side. We agreed we wanted nothing to do with them. Leaning towers of ice in the middle made us nervous because we couldn't see a safe way to traverse above or below them. The left side also looked problematic, with a steep jumble of hard packed snow, towering blocks of ice, and pouting lips of crevasses. A convoluted route, around rock bands lower down, and then up a boulder-strewn ridge along the left side of the face, looked to be the safest bet.

The American teams that passed us a week before had already re-treated, but below us, camped on a rock ledge under an overhang, were eight Polish climbers. We'd met them at basecamp. They were playing hooky. Poland had its own iron curtain then, but they'd convinced the government that it should be a matter of national pride that Poles ascend the Polish Route for the fiftieth anniversary of the first ascent. As long as they were on the route, they didn't have to go back to martial law, so they'd been there for weeks living on supplies abandoned by other expeditions, as well as a prodigious store of sausages, garlic, and root vegetables. Their leader was Wojchiech. He was tall with blonde hair and could speak English. With a friendly smile, he invited us to dinner. We stood around a wood stove they'd fabricated from slabs of rock while the stocky cook, Adam, shoved in pieces of mesquite and monitored a hissing pressure cooker. He had a mustache and a mischievous grin and dared us to eat cloves of raw garlic.

Our plan was to acclimatize at the toe of the Polish Glacier, and then climb along the left side of the face to the summit ridge where we would put in a high camp. We were stuck when a third blizzard swept in. After the wind died, we milled around the outside of the tent to see if breaking camp was in the cards. I grabbed my shovel and walked downhill to our latrine, chopped out chunks of wind slab packed hard against a tongue of ice, bashed the chunks into a sugary snow, and shoveled over the ugly part.

When I looked up, four Poles shuffled in formation through some boulders toward the bottom of the face. Dave thought it must be a desperate summit move, but that seemed impossible to me. After an hour, two peeled off and started up the middle between walls of ice. We caught glimpses as they climbed a diagonal line up the face. In late afternoon we heard a moan and high winds roared back in. Within minutes, a ground blizzard obscured everything. I wrapped a scarf around my head so I could stay outside.

When two Poles emerged from the whiteout, they told us Wojchiech and Adam had pressed on. I imagined our mountain friends holed up in a crevasse on the face, wrapping arms around each other to stay warm. Light faded as the Poles stood between boulders and cried "Adam," "Wojchiech." Then the cries stopped.

At two in the morning Terry shook me awake.

"I hear voices."

"OVER HERE, OVER HERE," he shouted.

Dave and I scrambled to pull on our climbing boots and anoraks. We didn't take time to strap on crampons, but grabbed ice axes and water bottles. I switched on my headlamp and moved up between some boulders. Dave went to my left around a small rock tower. The blizzard had plastered everything with snow and ice. A shadow moved out from behind a boulder into my headlamp's cone of light. Wojchiech. He didn't have a lamp and was shuffling because he had lost a crampon. He spoke rapidly in Polish while gesturing over his shoulder, until I grabbed his arm and started guiding him toward the Pole's camp. After a hundred yards, his knees sagged. I propped him up and handed him my water bottle. He took a drink and dropped the bottle. I swiped at it but it accelerated out of my headlamp beam down an icy slope. Dave called out from behind that he'd found Adam.

"YO, POLE'S CAMP, YO, POLE'S CAMP," I shouted.

A climber with a scarf wrapped around his face came out from the Polish tents and took Wojchiech by the arm. Adam moved past. As I turned, Dave shouted.

"WHOAA."

He lay flat on his stomach with the pick of his ice axe dug in for self-arrest. It was only then I recognized how precarious we were on a slippery slope without crampons. I used my ice axe to chop steps over to Dave, helped him to his feet, and started chopping steps toward our camp. When we finally stumbled into the tent, Terry had hot water going. I coughed and coughed between gulps of tea.

The next morning a huge lenticular cloud swirled around the upper face like a hive of angry bees. We walked over to the Pole's camp and learned Wojchiech had stumbled over the body of the frozen climber on his descent. Without a headlamp he didn't know what it was until he fumbled around in the dark and felt a frozen arm sticking straight up.

No wonder he was babbling.

The Poles told us they were breaking camp. They'd wearied of viento blanco and had all the time in the world to wait at Plaza Argentina for better weather. We debated what to do. I'd promised to be back in a month and lobbied to stay high.

"The weather pattern has to change," I said. "We'll be in the best position for a summit bid when it does."

Terry didn't know better. He'd never been at that altitude. Dave didn't care. He was going on to Chile after we descended anyway. But, the storm pattern didn't change. Each day, there was an interlude when we almost convinced ourselves it was over, but then the wind would roar back in and blow from all directions. Most hours we were in a stupor leaning against poles, slumping over in pathetic attempts to sleep, waking to brace against another gust, or dashing outside to chop wind slab for making water on the sputtering stove. I kept coughing and coughing. One night, I felt the first uneasy qualms of diarrhea. By the morning, they had turned into explosive discharges. Again and again I struggled out of the tent, ran to the latrine in my climbing boots while trying to unzip and drop my bibs. Dave came back from his own visit with a grim look.

"It looks like you've been doing strafing runs over there," he said.

My hacking got worse, my ribs hurt, and I woke up each time I coughed. Dave and Terry took turns checking my heartbeat and listening for fluid in my chest. In my waking state, I kept thinking about Beth's fountain of warmth whenever I let her be close. I wanted to bury my face between her breasts, for her to stroke my hair. One night in a vivid high altitude dream, I asked her to marry me. She hesitated and then said no. The shock I felt in the dream brought me to a waking state. I switched on my headlamp and scratched in my journal.

What madness is this? Is love your greatest risk or is risk your greatest love?

The wind stopped on the morning of the eighth day. I lay on my back while Dave measured my heartbeat at rest. It was ten beats higher than it had ever been. Dave said he wanted to step out of the tent to talk. He didn't have to tell me why. We both knew it could be an early sign of high altitude pulmonary edema.

"You need to go down," he said.

I looked up at the face. Sun shone on it for the first time in weeks. Lenticular clouds drifted away from the pyramid like flying saucers. I knew Dave would want to do the right thing, and in doing it he and Terry would lose their shot at the summit.

"If you go down with me, you'll never make it back up here," I said.

We stared at each other. I wrapped my arm around his shoulder and looked closely in his eyes.

"I can get down."

I grabbed some food and coffee, rolled up our blue tarp, stuffed everything into my pack, shook hands with Dave and Terry, and said I would leave a note at basecamp. When I started down with crampons strapped on, they were dropping the tent. The steep slopes were plastered with hard ice. Rocks and boulders on the talus slopes glinted like giant glass balls. I felt unsteady and moved slowly. Each plant of a ski pole, each step with a crampon, brought tightness to my throat. My instinct was to keep moving until I found the Poles. Hours later, in fading light, Wojchiech and Adam stood by the trail. They'd watched me descend the steep slopes into the nieves penitentes, and Adam had heated up borscht with sausages floating in it. Wojchiech helped me set up the blue tarp into an A-frame stretched over my ski poles. The Poles had a team doctor, and Wojchiech translated while the doctor listened to my lungs and said I had bronchitis.

In the morning, my mood was sour. I put on my hiking boots and wandered the cornrows of moraine. Incensed at the turn of events, I second-guessed every choice we'd made, and wondered in my journal if the mountain gods had gotten personal.

Why was I denied entry into the hall of the mountain king?

In early afternoon, the fact that it was over fifty kilometers to the highway and I had only two days of food started weighing on my mind. I shook hands with Wojchiech and handed him a note for Dave that I would wait in Mendoza, a colonial city two hundred kilometers east in the foothills of the central Andes. My pack was top heavy, with climbing boots and tarp strapped on, the trail was steep and rocky, and I was wobbly on my feet. Even with my ski poles I kept stumbling. Twisting an ankle, I pitched forward, screaming in pain, and dragged ahead on my forearms. An hour later it happened again. As night closed in I reached a spring spilling out of a rock wall. I stuck my face in and drank until I had to come up for air and then soaked my swollen ankles. A nearby granite boulder presented an opportunity for the tarp to be rigged as a lean-to. I set it up and crawled under.

An American expedition moved up during the night and pitched tents around the boulder. In the morning I waved to clean-shaven young men in new orange and yellow mountain suits and offered them cowboy coffee made over a mesquite fire. I said the coffee had come all the way from Alaska. When they stared and shook their heads, I looked down at my climbing bibs. The normally bright red legs were dirty purple and stained with brown streaks.

I reached the highway in the pass after the sun had set behind the western mountains. My plan was to hitchhike to Puente del Inca, but across the highway from the trailhead was a military installation I hadn't noticed when we'd met the gauchos. We'd left our passports with Fernando, and I thought of trying to sneak by, but there was no way to avoid being seen. I stashed my pack by the side of the road, walked across a parking area to a low-slung structure with mortared rock walls and a slate tile roof, and pushed in a heavy wooden door with a sign that said "Hombres." Next to a urinal, a dark skinned soldier with coal black hair sat at a beaten up metal desk smoking a cigarette. His belly bulged out between the buttons of his blue tunic. On his right sleeve were three yellow stripes. He looked me up and down with a toothy smile. I nodded and turned to look in a dirty mirror. My weathered cheeks looked sunken, my beard scraggly, and long greasy hair stuck out in all directions. I washed my hands and face and peaked over my shoulder. The sergeant was looking at some papers. I tied a blue bandanna over my hair, nodded again, and strode for the door. As it closed, I heard him talking excitedly in Spanish. I kept moving. Another soldier in a blue uniform came out of a low building and started shouting. I turned to face him. He held an AR-15 in one hand with the muzzle pointed in the air. His brown eyes burned. The only Spanish I knew I'd learned from a thin paperback on the long plane ride to Buenos Aires. I started backing toward the highway with my palms up.

"Norteamericano."

He brought the AR-15 down into both hands.

"Estoy andiniste."

He shouted again.

"Voy a expeditione Aconcagua."

Out of the corner of my eye an old fuel truck approached on the highway. The brakes squealed as it stopped behind me. The driver said a few Spanish words in a conversational tone to the soldier, who spun on his heels and walked away. The driver motioned me to get in. I stepped up on the running board and climbed onto the passenger seat.

"Gracias."

He had dark skin and a weathered face like the gauchos and looked at me with a weary smile.

"Punta del Inca?"

Two days later I checked into a hotel in Mendoza boasting that the Presidente had stayed there. Every day the sky was cloudless and temperatures were in the eighties. Each afternoon I lay by a rooftop pool. Whenever I got sweaty and rose to dive in, Argentine men with prodigious bellies and their bejeweled wives stared at my emaciated body. I had lost over twenty pounds. A week later Dave and Terry stepped off a red bus with bright chrome bumpers. They'd staggered through a snowstorm up a long ridge before arriving at what they thought was the summit.

"There was nothing else but air," Dave said. "When we turned to leave the snow had filled in our tracks."

Days later I arrived in Juneau on a late plane from Seattle. Beth felt my ribs.

"You're just a shell of your former self."

She drove her Rambler into downtown and we walked up a flight of stairs to her apartment. I lay on the bed and reached for her. Six weeks later, when Mitch was on another business trip, she spent the night at my house with a pregnancy test kit. In the morning she stepped out of the bathroom.

"It came out blue," she said. "I'm sure it happened the night you got back."

We looked at each other for a long time. I had been through an abortion, holding the woman's twitching head in my hands while a doctor probed with a suction tool beneath a yellowing sheet. It was one of the worst experiences of my life.

"I don't want you to get an abortion," I said.

"I don't want to be a single mom again."

All day I thought about how much my life was going to change. That evening we went to a dockside restaurant. The waiter seated us by a window overlooking Gastineau Channel. I fiddled with my white cloth napkin while talking about not owning a car, Mitch having to find someplace else to live, and colleagues getting used to my new status.

"It'll take time to make adjustments," I said.

During a long pause Beth studied my face.

"I want you to ask me."

"What?"

"I want you to ask me."

She brushed back her hair. Her dark brown eyes were deep pools and every muscle in her moon shaped face was taut. The ritual I had avoided for so long was at hand.

STRANGERS

B eth and I made our vows before a minister who referred to her as "having great courage" after I told him about the grizzly charge and her finger getting caught in the tram pulley. The only day that worked for the wedding was my fortieth birthday, and I thought I'd at least never have to forget about remembering our anniversary. Nine-year old Natalie was the ring bearer, and Beth wore a loose fitting pink dress to cover up that she was four months pregnant. On our honeymoon, we talked about how time was running out for us to paddle another remote river before the baby was born. I promoted the Noatak River in northwest Alaska. From a drop-off at a pond near its headwaters, it traverses west through the Brooks Range for three hundred and fifty miles to the Inupiaq village of Noatak. On a fine August day five years earlier, I'd flown down the Noatak with a buddy in his small plane and thought it traversed some of the wildest country left in Alaska. When I told Beth the Western Arctic Caribou Herd, then nearly two hundred thousand strong, should cross the river in August on its migration south, the deal was cinched. We hoped for something similar to the intimate encounters we'd had with bears on the Andreafsky.

I relished our preparations for what could be a month in the wilderness. We met with Beth's obstetrician Sarah, who grew up in Fairbanks and spent a lot of time in the bush. Our proposal to paddle the river while Beth was six months pregnant didn't alarm her, but she said it would be good if we had a way to reach out if a problem developed. Most pilots flying small planes in Alaska in those days monitored a standard emergency frequency, so I purchased a hand held two-way radio at a Boeing Field store during a trip to Seattle.

"I can beam up to a plane flying down the river," I told Beth.

Beth cut out the front of her new red river pants and sewed in a patch of blue stretch fabric to accommodate an expanding belly. I purchased a stainless steel .44 magnum pistol and a shoulder holster so I could carry it while we paddled. Our two-person Klepper kayak was also new, a wedding present to us from me, and we practiced loading it to make sure our food and camping gear could fit in its tight spaces. Our cans of fish and food bags and boxes would have to be stashed inside the hull by our thighs, so we carefully planned our food. I thought we would be fine. I'd heard the Noatak had abundant populations of grayling and arctic char, and I planned to fish every day. In the central Brooks Range village of Bettles, when we boarded a red floatplane to fly two hours west to the Noatak's headwaters, I thought we had everything we needed.

We've planned for everything.

What I didn't count on was my past taunting me. A past I had almost forgotten. On the Noatak, I re-learned Faulkner's truth: "The past is never dead. It isn't even the past."

When I was in my twenties, my best friend Sumner built a small log cabin on Lake Clark, a fifty-mile long freshwater fjord in southwest Alaska. The cabin sat close to a beach surrounded by wilderness. Sumner could land there in his modified cobalt blue bush plane he called the "Mystery Ship," which he claimed could fly slower than any other plane in Alaska. That was before Lake Clark and its surrounding mountains and hills north of even more immense Lake Iliamna were made a national park: the area was well known for dramatic scenery and abundant populations of wildlife.

Sumner buzzed my Hope cabin with the Mystery Ship in September of 1974. I drove up to the landing strip in my flatbed, where he stood by the plane with his girlfriend Claire, a short young woman with reddish hair tied behind her head. It was the first time we'd met and she greeted me with a stunning smile. Sumner was tall, six-foot-four, and missing a front tooth that had been gone since we were in high school in Fairbanks. He leaned forward and dropped his chin while telling me they were worried about out-of-state hunters killing big game animals for their heads in a vast band of hills west of Nondalton, a traditional Dena'ina village near the southern end of Lake Clark. He and Claire intended to use the Lake Clark cabin as a home base for spying on the hunters and guides.

"The guides advertise all-species hunts for ten grand, and promise you can get them in a week," he said.

I'd hunted since I was a kid growing up outside Fairbanks, and still enjoyed shooting waterfowl and grouse on the wing as much as the next guy, but hunting for big animals for me was only about bringing home the meat, which usually involved a lot of work.

"Who would want to go to the trouble of killing a moose, caribou, grizzly, and Dall sheep ram all in one week?" I asked.

"Rich men, some women. A lot are European. They don't really do any work," he said.

Claire said they'd be gone four or five days and invited me along. I jumped at it. I loved flying with Sumner in the Mystery Ship, and I'd never been to Lake Clark. In the morning we took off from Hope, flew west over the Kenai Mountains and across Cook Inlet, through glaciated and snow-capped mountains rimming Lake Clark Pass, and down a muddy river to the jade green end of upper Lake Clark. The Mystery Ship bounced up and down a rocky beach before Sumner brought it to a stop. We tied it down to some boulders, and walked to a small cabin with a tarpapered roof almost hidden in the trees behind a point protruding into the lake. That night Sumner told me hunting guides had built lodges in Nondalton next to the Dena'ina village. He knew two sisters who lived in the village, Liz and June, and he wanted me to meet them.

"They're watching first hand what's going on," he said.

It was mid-morning when we arrived in Nondalton. The gravel landing strip was located on a hill above the private lodges on the lakeshore. The landing strip seemed enormous to me. Sumner said it was on private land and had been enlarged so several planes from Anchorage could unload hunters at the same time. We walked over to the only building, a screened-in shed sitting next to a gravel road going downhill toward the lake. Inside were two moose quarters hanging on manila ropes from a beam.

"The village meat shed," Sumner said.

He told me meat from whatever the guides and hunters brought back was hung to age in the shed. I opened a screen door and stepped inside. The quarters were cool and the skin had a stiff purpling crust. Perfect for eating.

"Can anyone cut some off?" I asked.

Sumner paused while chewing the end of his mustache.

"Ask Liz or June," he replied.

The gravel road to the lake led straight to the private hunting lodges. They weren't fancy on the outside, faded log and rough lumber construction, but they had big decks on the lake and docks for tying up multiple float-planes. We took another gravel road into the Dena'ina village, and walked along until we stood before a sprawling log cabin. Liz and June invited us in for tea. They were beautiful young Dena'ina women with long black hair and flashing brown eyes. Sumner and Claire engaged Liz, and all three were laughing when I asked June if people in the village had much contact with the lodges. She said her boyfriend Danny was an assistant guide and pilot for one. When I asked if it was okay to walk around the village, she said she'd go with me. At the end of my tour we walked up the hill to the landing strip and stood by the meat shed. I noticed that no one from the lodges or the village could see us standing there, so I pulled a joint out of my shirt pocket, lit it with a match, and handed it to June. She gave me a broad, toothy smile, took a drag, and handed it back.

"Does your family get meat out of the shed?" I asked.

She nodded and I handed her the joint again.

"Can anyone in the village get meat there?"

"You have to ask," she replied.

"What do you mean?"

"You can't just take any. You have to get permission."

"Did your family have to ask?"

Her smile vanished. She shook her head and looked down the gravel street. When Sumner and Claire came into view, she walked toward them and waved goodbye over her shoulder. The Mystery Ship was still climbing out from the Nondalton strip when I shouted over the engine noise.

"WHAT IF YOUR DAUGHTER DOESN'T FUCK A GUIDE?"

Sumner shrugged and banked the Mystery Ship west toward hills draped in gold hued tundra. Within minutes we flew over a Super Cub sitting on a tundra-covered bench above a small lake. A bull moose fed in willows along the edge of the lake, and a hunter in camouflage clothing was sneaking up on it.

"Another same day airborne kill," Sumner said with an exasperated voice.

He didn't have to explain. Spotting big game animals from a plane and landing to shoot them was illegal in Alaska. It had been for years.

"This was not supposed to happen. I talked to Danny just a few days ago. He told me things were going to be different."

We flew on for a few more minutes and saw another Super Cub on the tundra. It was Danny's plane. Sumner dipped the Mystery Ship down and buzzed it. Two faces looked up as we flew on deeper into the hills, where we saw more Super Cubs on the ground. In late afternoon we headed back toward Nondalton, flying fifty feet above the beach along a convoluted lake shore, banking left when the shore zigged east, banking right when it zagged west. I had been in the Mystery Ship before with Sumner when he had done this kind of flying. It was his way of making a grand entrance.

We banked hard around a point and the private lodges were right off our wingtip. I looked out my side and saw three men standing on a weathered deck staring at us with drinks in their hands and mouths agape. A huge plane on floats sat below us at a dock. Burly men in sweatshirts muscled moose heads with bloody necks into the back. Sumner banked the Mystery Ship hard toward the landing strip, touched down, and jammed on the brakes. He jumped out and ran down the gravel road to the beach.

"DANNY," he shouted, "YOU SAID THIS WAS GOING TO STOP."

All I could hear was a grunted response. I looked in the meat shed. The same two quarters that had been there in the morning were still there. Nothing more. Sumner quickly walked back up to the strip with an angry look on his face. That evening in his cabin, we sat on spruce rounds around a kerosene lamp. Sumner obsessed about Danny lying to him. Claire, who I'd learned in just one day was smart and tuned into old time Alaska, was outraged at the sheer waste. My mind dwelled in a very dark place, where trophy hunters acted like excited kids in a shooting gallery, and the only meat saved was for families with beautiful daughters. Even months later, I could still find that dark place.

Over the next decade the Trans-Alaska Pipeline came and Alaska boomed, the State started handing out checks called "dividends," and my buddy Sumner was killed in a mid-air collision. I saw his death as the line demarking what Alaska was and what it would become. Memories of what was shrunk away in my mind like an old friend disappearing in a rear-view mirror. Until eleven years later on the Noatak.

We were in scenic mountainous terrain and the weather was shirt-sleeve warm, but things didn't go as planned from the beginning. Beth's lower back went into spasm while bending over to push Klepper parts into place. We shoved off, but soon we were camped along a river slough where she could float on her back with arms stretched overhead, trying to relieve the pain. We started downriver again, but then stopped so she could lie on a foam pad and stretch. I tied a runner to a willow bush, and she reached overhead to hold onto it while I held her heels in my hands and leaned back as far as I could. We didn't cover many miles a day because of stops for traction and stretching. All the while, the river was low and I searched for a grayling at every stop in vain.

After a week of slow progress, Beth's back improved. We left the bigger mountains behind and moved out into a basin. Black clouds dominated upriver when our bow skidded onto a narrow gravel beach at the base of a steep gravel bank. We carried gear and food up to a broad rocky shelf. Beth started looking for a place to set up the tent while I returned to the beach to tie the lines of the kayak to some big rocks. A strange voice startled me and I spun around. A short man stepped out from behind a willow thicket. He had a round face and a reddish beard, and wore a dark wool jacket, blue jeans, and leather boots scuffed almost grey. The pupil of his right eye seemed to wander around. I wasn't happy with the idea of meeting a stranger in the wilderness.

"What? Where did you come from?" I asked.

He pointed with his chin upriver toward a small raft resting on top of the bank next to an alder bush.

"Do you need help carrying your kayak up the bank?" he asked.

Does he think I don't know what I am doing?

"No, I've taken care of it," I replied.

He nodded and walked back upriver. When I looked over later, he had pitched a small tent. By then, Beth had asked if the kayak was safe, and I was reconsidering the situation.

We ARE out in the middle of a basin, and it IS raining upriver.

I walked over to look across the river. The opposite bank looked like the one on our side, steep gravel with recent evidence of higher river levels. From my vantage point the channel below me looked like it was in a trough, and it dawned on me that all of the water coming down from the basin upriver funneled through that trough during heavy rains. I walked down and started dragging the kayak up the bank. By the time I made it to the top and tied the kayak to some willows I was hot and sweaty. When I pulled off my rain jacket to cool down, the little guy stood up and waved.

Over the next few days we leapfrogged past each other. He was faster getting out of camp than we were, but we cruised downriver faster, so he'd pass us in the morning and we'd pass him late in the afternoon. He waved every time and I started waving back. He pulled over one morning. Beth had taken off her raincoat. When she reached to grab his raft and pull it into the beach, her pregnant belly bulged out the blue stretch fabric she'd sewn into her red river pants. His name was Mike and he was on vacation from his job as a mental health counselor in Kotzebue. Beth said I'd had trouble catching grayling.

"I'll keep a look out for arctic char when I'm ahead of you," he said in a soft voice as his raft drifted away.

Black clouds moved in, the temperature dropped, and rain swept downriver. The only shelter we found one afternoon was a bank jutting out where the river had undermined it. It was time for lunch when we nosed the kayak into a slope of soft wet silt and climbed up to roots hanging down like a string curtain. Beth pushed them aside so I could scrape out a spot where we sat side-by-side behind them. The roots swayed in the wind and water poured off the lip while we set up the camp stove and Beth heated water for instant chicken noodle soup. I spread cream cheese and raspberry jam on water crackers and handed them to her. I felt guilty taking as much as I did. The fishing had been so slow we were already rationing food. That evening we decided to wait out the storm and hunkered down in our tent close to a small stream. When it broke in late afternoon two days later, temperatures were ten degrees colder and the edges of willow leaves had turned a lemony yellow.

Mike's raft came into view the next morning when I was cooking breakfast over a willow fire. I waved him in to our camp. He tied up next to us and sat on a tube while Beth handed him plates of steaming pancakes with butter and syrup. He told us he'd started out hunting for moose, but changed his mind when he discovered the system he had envisioned for elevating meat above the wet floor of his raft wouldn't really work. If the meat couldn't stay dry, he didn't think it could properly cool and didn't want any to go to waste.

"Now, I'm just sightseeing," he said.

I asked him if he was from Kotzebue. He shook his head.

"I grew up in Iliamna."

"I flew around Lake Iliamna and Lake Clark in the seventies," I said. "There were a lot of trophy hunters back then."

"That's one reason I ended up in Kotzebue."

I could see in his face a weary and sad look. A look I thought I had seen before. Someone displaced from his or her homeland by the onslaught of outside greed. It occurred to me that floating the Noatak for him was akin to going home again, where moose and caribou were plentiful and airplane hunters hadn't taken over. Before Mike shoved off, we agreed to keep tabs on each other while going downriver.

When the river entered steep hills blanketed with golden tundra, the Western Arctic Caribou Herd came visiting. We had pitched our tent on the south side of the river at the top of a dirt bank thick with willows. It was a clear morning and I was on my back in the tent enjoying the top light up from the rising sun. I heard splashing, thought it must be a bear, and scrambled outside. Across the river, caribou dove one after another off a steep bank into deep water, white collars flashing each time one hit the sun's rays, and swam for our side. The rack of the lead caribou bobbed in the current on top of a brown face and black nose and headed straight toward our camp. When it saw us peaking through the willows, it snorted, turned its head downriver, and swam toward a hole in the bank where it had collapsed into the river. It thrust its two front legs onto the pile of silt, bounded up, shook off water like a dog, drops glinting in the sun, and leaped up the bank. The rest followed, until a line of racks bobbed all across the channel, with one bounding out of the water on our side, and another diving off the bank on the north side.

During our second cup of coffee, the caribou stream turned into a trickle, but the trickle kept up all morning and into the afternoon. By the time we shoved off, all that was left was a deep trail beaten into the silt up the bank. We paddled rhythmically downriver while caribou bands continued to cross. In camp, I looked at our maps and realized we had covered over fifteen miles in two hours. If we could make that kind of progress each day, we might have enough food. Traction and yoga had helped Beth's back recover, but I worried the spasm might flare again.

"Was this too much?" I asked.

She shook her head.

"My back's better, my abdominals feel strong, and the baby only kicked once."

I thought for a moment.

"The herd is going to continue crossing. How about we just load the kayak, hang out watching until late afternoon, and then stroke downriver?"

"I'd love to see more like today," she said.

We spent the next few days lingering along gravel bars while Beth stretched and did yoga on her foam pad, waiting for bands of caribou to spill over the tops of the hills. When we spotted a band streaming down golden hillsides like undulating rivulets toward the river, we drifted to a spot where we thought they would cross and stood by. One afternoon on the north shore, we crouched in some willows at the base of a steep silt bank and held the lines on each end the kayak. I thought it seemed like the caribou were taking a long time, so I stuck my head up to peak around. A bull with an enormous rack peered down over the edge of the bank. A variegated shovel on his antlers pointed right at my head, and we were so close I could see moisture around the edges of his black nose. I sucked in my breath and ducked down. The bull snorted and jumped back. Other caribou behind him kept moving, split into two streams on each side of us, and plunged into the river. The clack, clack, clack sound of hooves and the click, click, click sound of joints mingled with splash, splash, splashing into the river. They brushed by only feet and sometimes, just inches, away. I caught whiffs of a pungent smell and marveled at how they managed to avoid us in the chaos. The last calf lagged behind, and ran up and down our side until it tentatively entered the river. Almost immediately it started losing a struggle against a strong current. A large cow wheeled around, bounded back into the channel, positioned herself downstream of the calf, and nudged it across with her nose. The large bull jumped down the bank on Beth's side, and other bulls followed. Within minutes, their white rumps disappeared into the brush on the other side of the river. We shoved off and drifted while bands of caribou, some in the hundreds, continued to stream down hills to the north of the river and up hills to the south. It felt like we were in a lavish dream where the sky and hills and caribou and river were painted with the bold use of blue and gold and brown and grey by the likes of a van Gogh.

A day later we saw a red and white floatplane land at an ox-bow lake close to the river. Then I heard rifle shots. The following evening we camped at the first good site we'd seen in hours. Our yellow dome tent was pitched on a sandy spot close to the river's edge, a tangle of driftwood was right next to us and we had a good fire going, its yellow flames reflecting off the grey hull of the kayak. I was squatting by the fire when I looked upriver. A small green canoe with a solo paddler emerged from the dull greyness of dusk and bank and bar and water. I stood up. I had seen canoes like it before, a twelve-foot inflatable made in Germany, big enough for one paddler, camping gear, and carefully thought out food. A camouflage spray cover stretched oddly over something in the bow. As the canoe neared, I realized that forked tines of caribou antlers under the spray cover were pushing it up like so many tent poles.

There's no room in that canoe for the meat to go with those antlers.

My mind flashed to the floatplane in Nondalton stuffed with moose heads.

Trophy hunter.

The paddler maneuvered toward a shallow spot right next to our fire and grabbed some willows to hold the canoe in the current. A broad billed hat shadowed his face. All I could see in the light from the fire were the tips of his chin and nose.

"I haf been on the river eighteen hours," he said in a guttural accent.

A primal rage rose up inside me.

He's left meat behind and now he wants us to share our camp?

I stepped in front of the fire and cast a shadow over him.

"Then you better keep moving. It's going to be dark before long."

He sat motionless as if trying to comprehend. I wanted him to feel unwelcome, even insulted, so I turned my back and started tossing more driftwood on the fire. When I heard the canoe scrape against willows, I turned to see him drift downriver and disappear into the blankness of evening. Beth's eyes flashed in the light of the fire.

"Why did you treat him that way?"

I told her about the antlers under the spray cover, trophy hunters leaving the meat, and the plane stuffed with moose heads.

"For them it's all about the killing," I said.

"I don't like that either, but he was a human being asking for help."

She turned away in the tent when I tried to put my arms around her. In the morning she spent a long time looking at the river.

"When I see you like you were last night, I ask myself 'who is this stranger I just married?'"

I started to blurt out "he made his choice," but thought better of it. A day later we saw Mike again.

"A trophy hunter tried to come into our camp just as it was getting dark," I said. "I didn't let him near our fire."

"I didn't like the way Doug treated him at all," Beth said.

Mike shook his head.

"Someone else told me yesterday about meat left to rot."

When we paddled out of the steep hills, we left the Western Arctic herd behind us and lost track of Mike for a few days. Was he ahead of us? Still upriver? I wondered about my rage and hoped Beth's memory of it would soften if I said nothing more about trophy hunters. Horizons opened up, northern harriers flitted above gravel bars, and peregrine falcons rapidly flapped their wings overhead. The tundra turned a deep red, every morning brought ice in the water pot, and our food dwindled to scraps. I tried to snag red-sided dog salmon spawning in shallow pools but didn't have the right hooks, and they kept finning away. I knew the confluence with the Kelly River was coming up and told Beth about some friends bringing back dozens of arctic char after a day fishing there.

"We'll catch a lot of fish at the Kelly," I said.

A day above the Kelly, Mike reappeared. He'd spotted us eating the last of our salami and crackers on a gravel bar. When Beth told him I had been trying to snag salmon, he reached down and lifted up a spawned out dog salmon with faded red sides, half a tail, and a green toothy head. He held it out with both hands and gave Beth a shy look. His right eye looked at me. I wanted to decline, but all we had left was some dry pasta and a little cheddar cheese.

"We wondered what we were going to eat," Beth said.

She gave him a warm smile. He grinned and bowed his head. When Mike rowed his raft back out into the current, I looked forward to celebrating with him at the Kelly with fresh char cooked on our camp grill. I didn't know the outline of him looking downriver, stretching up in his seat so he could see deeper into the bend, would be the last we would ever see of him.

ARCTIC CHAR

Beth is seven months pregnant. We're camped on a barren gravel bar in the western Brooks Range, three hundred miles downriver from where we launched our kayak. We've been on rations for over a week. We need fresh meat.

I convinced her we would catch lots of fish. But, the Noatak was low from the start. I caught only one grayling, and it was not much more than a mouthful apiece. During the second week it was two hours a day for a mouthful apiece. Two days ago, I spotted a flash of color in a small pool as we drifted by the mouth of a stream.

Red flash, maybe it's a char's belly.

It was a dog salmon with green fingers groping red sides. I tried to snag it with my biggest spoon but it kept finning away. The next day I saw another, but it kept finning away too. In late afternoon, Mike, our friend we had made on the river, presented Beth with a spawned out dog salmon with a green back, a big toothy nose, and half a tail left. When I laid it on a bed of grass in the bottom of the kayak, she arched her eyebrow. The flesh was white and mushy, but we ate it for dinner.

And now, another day downriver, I'm scrambling from one pool to another across a broad floodplain, searching the clear waters of the Kelly River for an arctic char. At the highest pool, a flash appears behind my spoon and then is gone.

Silver, not red.

I cast again. The line shudders. When I lift the rod tip, a hefty arctic char breaks the surface. My tackle is light and the fish is strong. The char surges, the drag screams, and I let it run, trying to keep it from the fast current or wrapping the line around a willow. When it stops, I gently reel in. But, then it runs again and I have to start over.

My wrist aches but I have managed to work it to a tiny gravel beach. The char lies on its side in shallow water, its gills barely moving. I reach down and grab the line instead of the fish. The char flops, comes out of its stupor, and throws the hook.

NOOOOO!

The char slithers through shallow water. I dive with both hands outstretched. I can feel the char's smooth skin on my fingertips, can feel it slip from my hands. It's gone. I stand up and look down river. Beth stretches on a foam pad, her pregnant belly a bump in the flat landscape of the river bar. I can't face her yet. Noatak Village is still two days down river.

SHELIKOF SOLSTICE

I heard gurgling and sat up. Infant Charley and ten-year-old Natalie slept between us. When I unzipped the tent door and scanned outside into burgeoning twilight, the quiet meandering stream we'd camped next to during the storm enveloped us like a moat. I couldn't figure out what had happened, but we were surrounded, and it looked like the water was still rising.

"Beth, wake up, we have to move now."

She peeked out, gave me a wide-eyed look, and got busy with me. We slipped Charley into his one-piece suit and dropped his feet through the holes in our baby backpack. Natalie pulled on her yellow raingear and black rubber boots. I stepped outside and scanned for higher ground.

It had all started as a good idea. Go to a Forest Service cabin outside of Sitka with Natalie, the shy ring bearer at our wedding, and Charley, eight months old and just crawling. It seemed like a chance for a benign family adventure. Our first since Beth and I returned from the Noatak. Beth's eyes brightened when I told her there were big ocean beaches on both sides of a cabin on Kruzof Island, a helicopter ride from the Sitka airport. Kruzof is thirty miles long, mountainous in the north and the south, with low grass-land in the middle called Iris Meadows, where the Shelikof River winds toward Shelikof Bay. South of the Shelikof River delta is a long sandy beach where a Forest Service cabin was located. The word was, at minus tides, we could access kelp draped rock formations from the beach that were usually submerged.

Beth said the first gillnetter opening of salmon season was always summer solstice when there were big tides and lots of fish. She got animated talking about finding abalone and digging razor clams on the biggest minus tides of the summer. She pushed hard to go during the third week of June. I agreed. I loved the idea of prying abalone off rocks and thought the beaches would be a safe place for the kids. A Juneau inventor was making a new kind of baby backpack, complete with a real harness and rain umbrella, and we got on his waiting list because he made them one at a time. During a Seattle trip, I went to an outdoor gear store on First Avenue and bought a top of the line four-person dome tent called a "North Star." It weighed twelve pounds, but it was designed to take any kind of weather during any season.

I called the District Ranger's office in Sitka and learned the cab-in was booked for Friday, Saturday, and Sunday on Solstice weekend. The beach was nearly a mile long and I thought we could camp at the far end until the cabin was available on Monday. We reserved Monday and Tuesday and packed for the trip. Our load was formidable: North Star tent, foam pads, sleeping bags, gas stove, steel pot, plastic dishes, food, rain gear, and extra clothes. Plus, five days of disposable diapers for Charley. I decided we should trim our load.

"Light is right," I told Beth.

"I've heard that before. What exactly do you propose?"

I said I was leaving fishing tackle, camera, binoculars, most of my extra clothes, and my running shoes. I convinced her we should only take one extra freeze-dried meal. My reasoning was that a helicopter could fly through most anything so it was unlikely there would be a weather delay on our return. I started going through the food and weighing each meal in my mind. When I got to mid-day snacks, Beth saw me counting crackers.

"Are you taking Natalie's appetite into account?"

Natalie was ten when she moved to Juneau to live with us before Charley was born. I thought she ate like a bird.

"I've never seen an adult eat more than ten crackers a day," I replied. "Ten a day times three people times five days is a hundred and fifty."

I bought Natalie a jackknife for the trip. Beth wasn't so sure.

"It's June," I said, "sap will be running in the willows. We can make a whistle together."

We left Juneau for Sitka on a warm cloudy day. Dark grey rain squalls drifted across Sitka Sound when we arrived, and the temperature was ten degrees colder. We took a cab to an outfit that had helicopters for charter. The pilot's name was Cecil. He wore a blue and white striped work shirt and his red suspenders held up loose fitting blue jeans. The tops of his rubber boots were rolled down, and you could see his white socks. His wife ran the office. She had a broad face and called him "Cec." Cec looked us over. We were all wearing quick dry clothes and rubber boots, but Natalie was small for a ten-year-old and Charley waved his arms all akimbo from the inventor's backpack.

"Weather on the outside of Kruzof is deteriorating," Cec said.

He scrunched his eyebrows like it was a question. I turned to Beth and Natalie.

"We need to put on rain gear now."

Cec nodded and loaded the helicopter. I sat in front. We crossed Sitka Sound and flew around the crater of Mt. Edgecumbe to the North Pacific coast of Kruzof. When Cec flew north along the beach where the Forest Service cabin was located, a four-wheeler track ran its entire length from the mouth of the Shelikof River to a big turnaround near a sea stack at the south end. I was stunned. I knew some folks from Sitka took four-wheelers on a trail from the east side of Kruzof to Iris Meadows, but it had never occurred to me they went all the way to the beach where the cabin was located. I had a visceral reaction to four-wheelers in those days. I grew up in Alaska before their use by city dwellers exploded, and in my mind they destroyed the peace and beauty of many places I had treasured. I pointed to the tracks and talked to Beth over the intercom system.

"We don't want to camp on a four-wheeler trail."

Cec hovered the helicopter and said over the intercom he could set us down on the next beach along the coast, beyond the Shelikof River and a rocky point jutting out. When the cabin was available, we could work our way back around the point to the cabin at low tide. I looked down. It was high tide and the mouth of the Shelikof River was a deep hole of green water.

"What about crossing the river?"

"It spreads out into shallow channels at low tide," Cec said.

Beth had a concerned look. I pointed toward the next beach, partially obscured in a squall, and Cec moved ahead. When the helicopter set down, sheets of rain splashed on the windshield. I jumped out and ducked my head.

"THERE'S A CREEK FURTHER ON," Cec shouted over the whistle of the rotor blades.

I looked in the direction he pointed. The sandy beach was narrow and snaked along the edge of a dense hemlock forest. I didn't see any sign of where a creek might come out. When the helicopter lifted off, we loaded Charley into the backpack and Beth helped me shoulder him on my back. I turned to keep the wind and rain out of his face. Strands of wet black hair spun in the wind around Natalie's yellow hood.

Beth and I agreed we needed to get to where we could hunker down, and that meant we had to be close to the stream. We grabbed a duffle apiece, and started down the beach. Rain was heavy, our loads were bulky, and the yellowish sand was loose. Natalie dragged her boots and dropped behind. I waited while Beth talked to her in a quiet voice and took her hand. When they caught up, Beth felt Charley's neck.

"He's cold," she said.

"We can find a spot to set the tent up and get him into a sleeping bag."

She shook her head.

"Let me take him."

I slipped off the backpack and carried Charley in front of me while Beth walked up the beach into the trees. She found a sheltered spot under the spreading limbs of a Western hemlock and sat on a giant root twisting across the top of the forest floor. She opened her raincoat, pulled up her long underwear top, and bared a full breast. I handed her Charley. His head bobbed up and down as his mouth grabbed her nipple. She pulled the sides of her coat together, held it with one hand, and looked up at me. Her face was calm.

"Go get another load."

"Really?"

She nodded. Natalie stood like a statute in her yellow raincoat as I walked away. When I returned with another duffle, she sat next to Beth, leaning across her lap, and Charley waved his arms. Beth looked up and smiled.

"It warmed him right up," she said.

"Maybe the best thing is for me to scout ahead while you stay here."

"Don't be gone too long."

I walked along the sodden beach while wind whipped spray off the tops of waves. A shallow stream came into view, spilling down the beach. I elected to stride up the middle of it along some meanders until I came to higher ground, a large patch of sand with a mound in the middle. I scraped around with my boots until there was a flat space as big as a living room. The water in the stream was clear, not stained brown from a muskeg swamp, and it was only a few feet away. The stream meanders reminded me in miniature of river channels Beth and I had camped along and I had a good feeling. When I brought Beth and the kids to look at it, she agreed. We hauled all the gear there, erected the North Star, fixed a pasta meal, and crawled into our sleeping bags.

When I realized the next morning we were surrounded by a moat, it was early twilight. I looked across the stream, now fifty feet wide, and saw what I thought was an otter slide dropping down a slope from a forested bench. In a hurry we stuffed the sleeping bags, deflated the sleeping pads, and packed the duffels. I picked up Natalie in both arms and plunged into slow moving current. The water was waist deep and I had to lift her up to my chin to keep her dry. Beth followed with Charley in the backpack. We crossed the channel and walked across a marshy meadow to dry ground. I put Natalie down and took Charley from Beth. She grasped Natalie's hand and led her up the trail to the top of the bench where there was a flat spot. It had been a campsite before and I wondered why I hadn't spotted it the previous afternoon. Beth huddled with Natalie and Charley while I went back for more loads.

The last thing to come up the bank was the North Star tent, which we left up in an attempt to keep it from getting soaked in the drumming rain. Natalie stayed with Charley while Beth and I carried it upside down, each gripping a side and holding it above our heads. It was unwieldy in the gusting wind and we had to move quickly across the moat, but we managed to carry it to the top of the bench with the floor only partly drenched. We tied it down, re-inflated the sleeping pads, and pulled the sleeping bags out of the stuff sacks. Only then did we sit on the edge of the bench and lift our feet up to drain our boots. Water poured out with vapor rising in the colder air. Beth and Natalie stripped down their rain gear and dove in. I handed in Charley.

"Aren't you coming in?" Beth asked.

"You get settled. If I come in now, I'll just get everything wet. I'll stay out for a while."

For most of the next two days I stood outside the tent while gusty winds and slashing rain moved through, cooking meals outside to hand in, and slipping in only when I was too tired to stand. Natalie ate like a horse and we started measuring out slices of cheese. She ran through her crackers and I gave her mine. I cut her a willow she could make into a whistle, but she sliced her finger open as soon as she tried. Beth used butterfly strips to close the wound. I carved a splint out of an alder branch and handed it in, and

Beth taped it to Natalie's finger so she wouldn't use it.

The wind died during the third night. Faint morning sun glimmered on a small lake as we walked to the outlet of the stream. Our previous campsite was under water with only a few rushes poking up. A bulging dune separated the lake from the beach, and we realized pounding wave action during the storm had plugged the mouth of the stream with sand.

"I remember our first gillnet openings often involved a storm," Beth said.

I tugged on her raincoat and laughed.

"When were you going to tell me?"

The lake was close to spilling over the top of the dune. Natalie and I took driftwood branches and tried to scoop out a trench for it to drain. It seemed like a futile exercise, but after a time with the lake rising and us periodically digging, a trickle started. The trickle turned into a stream and then a cascade. In the afternoon it was shallow when we waded across. We hiked back along the beach we had marched down in the rising storm. The tide was out when we picked our way around the point through kelp draped boulders. Instead of being braided, the Shelikof River was a broad channel with no indicators of where a ford might be. I picked Natalie up in both arms. She faced me and held on to my neck while I felt my way out to the main current with the toes of my boots. She looked back at her mom and Charley with every step. At one point I turned to face the current and crabbed across. Natalie looked into my eyes while I focused on the riffle in front of us. Finally, the current eased and we made it to a rocky beach. When I turned, Beth was already at the edge of the current with Charley on her back. I knelt down, took Natalie's hands in mine, and looked her in the eye.

"Can I leave you here and go help your mom?"

She got a shy look on her face and nodded. I moved crablike toward Beth, holding out my hand. She took it in the middle of the current and we shuffled toward Natalie. After one more crossing, we searched for the cabin. It was an A-frame, set back in the hemlock and dark inside, and there were mice, but it had a wood stove, a table and bunks, and a window that faced the direction we had come.

Two days later, the weather deteriorated, Cec didn't appear, and another couple showed up on a four-wheeler for the cabin. We vacated and set up camp near a sea stack a half-mile down the beach. I went back for the last load, a black trash bag full of dirty diapers. When the guy with the four-wheeler saw what I was doing, he took it from my hands and hauled it to our camp. That night we shared a freeze-dried meal generously called "chicken tetrazzini." It turned an ugly orange and smelled like dog food, but it was all we had left. I wanted to laugh when Natalie closed her eyes and pinched her nose to eat her share. ●

FALLING

Charley. I should have known you could stumble and fall. Even if I was only one step away. We just wanted to kill some time on a trail before Juneau's Fourth of July parade. How foolish of me to put you down where salmon berry bushes crowded it, camouflaging steep cliffs.

You start to roll. I grab for your sweatshirt and miss, dive and gather you into my arms, but we are already over the edge, funneled down a rocky avalanche chute, me on my back, head first, arms holding you tight to my chest.

We accelerate into a blur, branches and brush and loose rocks clawing at us, drop over the first ledge, airborne for an instant before my shoulders take the blow on loose rocks. My grip loosens, we brush a boulder, you bounce from my arms. I reach out, feel you with my right hand, pull you back to my chest. At the top of a bigger face, a longer fall.

I don't let go when we hit the bottom. You are still in my arms when I slide head first into a thicket of alders and stop. There isn't a sound. I see your tears and the bruise across your cheek, stroke your face, and hear your mom screaming "DOUG, DOUG" from above.

BLACK AND WHITE

In late August of 1985, when we drifted downriver in our kayak, we'd been on the Noatak for three weeks, but we were in no hurry for the trip to end, even if Beth was seven months pregnant.

"I'm in mourning," Beth said. "When will we be on a river again? When will life be so simple again as life is in a tent?"

After some thought, I said we should make up a song to the tune of "Little Grass Shack" and warbled the opening line.

"Take me, take me back to that little cloth shack on the Noatak."

Beth laughed and I challenged her to come up with the next line. She responded in tune.

"Tell me, tell me when we'll be back in the land of the midnight sun."

We sang the refrain over and over again until we beached the kayak at a muddy boat landing below the village of Noatak. We camped along a dirt road traversing up the side of a bluff to the village. Inupiaq women in bright calico parkas called atikłuks walked by and stared at Beth's swollen belly. Beth smiled and said hello and one invited us for tea. As we stood by the landing strip waiting for the mail plane, we vowed to return to the river.

Charley was born on a stormy day in Juneau. He had brown hair and his brown eyes were deep pools, just like his mom. He was three and already asking complicated questions when his brother Matt came along. Matt's hair was blond and I called him "our towhead." He was so strong he could lift his head off the bed on the day he was born.

When Matt was still in diapers, Beth and I made a deal. We would take the boys on wilderness river trips every year, and they would have music in their lives every day. We knew they both had to feel comfortable and unafraid in the water, so Beth took them to swimming lessons every week for years. During summers, we went car camping and learned the tent was a perfect venue for them building things with Legos, listening to stories, and playing cards. Whenever we were out where the only view was of a meadow or forest, and the only sound was the wind, Charley would get a serious look on his face and say, "Dad, I really love nature." Matt would always agree with a broad smile and yell "YEAH!"

I found an 18-foot collapsible Allypak canoe on sale that could carry a 1200 pound payload. We bought a stainless steel stand for a two-burner Coleman stove and a roll-up table so we wouldn't have to bend over while preparing meals. Our tent was the same North Star we had when Charley was an infant. Seven years after we vowed to return, Charley wore his hair in a long brown tail and read Archie comics. Matt had a buzz cut and was in constant motion. We strapped the canoe on top of our Toyota station wagon in Anchorage, loaded it with gear and a cooler, and drove north to Sourdough where there was a boat launch for the Gulkana River.

It was August, the hot sockeye salmon fishing was over, and cohos hadn't shown up yet, so the boat launch was deserted. By the time we were ready to shove off, it was late afternoon and thunderheads towered downriver. The boys sat side-by-side in the middle, with dry bags in front of them and behind. I tied a tarp to the forward thwart and folded it up at their feet. Beth climbed in front and sat in a lawn chair. My seat in the stern was the top of a cooler. We drifted so the boys could practice with short wooden paddles. Charley made a few good strokes and then stopped to look around. Matt splashed on the surface but kept at it.

An hour downriver, sheet lightning flashed overhead. Thunder cracked a heartbeat later. Light dimmed. The pungent smell of ozone filled the air. Rain poured out of a black sky. The river took on the same metallic grey hue as the rocks. I misread where a submerged boulder was in a shallow stretch. The bow of our canoe fetched up on it and we lurched to a stop.

"Beth, I'm going over the side."

She reached out with her paddle and braced the canoe. I vaulted out of the stern into thigh-deep water and found footing on a rocky bottom. Lightning lit the startled faces of Matt and Charley looking at me over their shoulders. I shoved, but the canoe didn't budge. Hail plunked into the current. I lifted the stern and shoved again. The canoe floated free.

"YOU'VE GOT THE BOAT," I shouted.

Beth and the boys paddled toward two spruce trees hanging off a dirt bank while I bellied in over the side, toes dangling in the current. When we slipped under the trees, Beth reached up and grabbed a spruce branch and I grabbed another. Gusts rocketed across the river and rocked the canoe. Hail, big as marbles, floated around my feet. Charley looked calm. Matt burst into tears.

"Oh, Matt honey, we're OK," Beth said in a soothing voice. "Dad's back in the canoe and we're all safe."

"Hey guys," I said, "grab the tarp."

They pulled it over their heads and ducked under. Beth and I held the canoe in place beneath the spruce trees. Thunder cracked above our heads. Charley peaked out his side. Lightning strobed on and off, and a gravel bar across the river looked like a black and white photo appearing and reappearing from behind a curtain. Matt fell asleep. Hail continued and slushy water rose four inches deep in the stern. I tipped up my sandals to take a look at my feet. My toes were wrinkled and white.

After an hour, the lightning and thunder and hail moved on. Charley and Matt stuck their heads out. Beth and I let go of the spruce branches and paddled across the current to the gravel bar where hail had drifted three inches deep. While Beth and I brushed off a spot for the tent with canoe paddles, the boys made little snowmen and threw snowballs, shrieking whenever they hit me in the back. In the tent we cuddled together while Beth read a story about a cave boy named Kip who met a wolf that became the first dog.

A wan sun peeked through breaks in the clouds the next day. By the time we shoved off, a stiff breeze blew in our faces. We tried to stay in the lee by hugging the river's edge along cut banks. When it didn't work, we'd get blown back upriver. After an hour, Beth pointed to a big gravel bar.

"Let's stop there and wait it out," she said.

I thought we might as well camp, and we pitched the tent downwind of a willow thicket. The lower end of the bar adjoined a swampy area of blueberry bushes and spindly black spruce. The boys ran over and started exploring. Pretty soon they were back.

"LOOK DAD," Matt shouted.

Charley held out a wood frog in his palm. It was no bigger than a half dollar, brown with yellow and black stripes on the side. Charley put it down and it leaped forward. Matt shrieked.

"I named it Leapy," Charley said.

He picked up Leapy and took it into the tent. For the next hour, while Beth and I bustled about, the boys played with Leapy. Every time it jumped, they both laughed as if it was the funniest thing they had ever seen. Matt started hugging him. When food was ready, Leapy was a little lethargic. Actually, Leapy was almost dead, so we convinced them to let it go.

That night, while we lay in our sleeping bags in the tent, I told a story I'd written in my journal while waiting out a five-day storm in the Alaska Range. In Three Boys and the Mountains, Doug and Charley and Matt find a secret passageway into a rock and ice castle in the Great Gorge of the Ruth Glacier. At the top of a long stairway they meet the Lord of the Moose's Tooth. He has wide eyes and long wavy hair the color of blue glacial ice, and a black beard that hangs straight down like a curtain. When I got to the part where the Lord gives the boys cookies, Charley sat up.

"Mom, I've got a loose tooth."

In the morning, it was blowing upriver. I had paddled the Gulkana before, and remembered a gravel bar a few miles downriver at the lower end of an ox-bow bend with hills on both sides of the river. I looked at my topographic map and thought a bluff across the river from that gravel bar might block the wind. We shoved off into gusty headwinds and struggled, all four paddling to make any progress. After two hours, we came to the bend. In the middle was a rocky stretch of whitewater with a tongue spilling over a ledge at the bottom. Beth used a draw stroke to align the bow with her paddle so the tongue pulled us straight toward a gravel beach where the river was still. She insisted we stay.

"It's just too much."

That evening, the boys clamored for Three Boys and the Mountains again, and when I was telling it, Charley's loose tooth came out.

"Mom, can the Tooth Fairy find me here on the river?"

"He can, but it will take him longer, probably tomorrow."

Beth told Charley to put his tooth in a mesh pocket on the inside of the tent. The wind died down during the night and in the morning there was warm sun for the first time. It was only five miles to the takeout, and Beth and the boys wanted to fish. She helped them rig their rods and they set off downstream to the beginning of a riffle. I pulled everything out of the tent, took the fly off, turned it upside down and shook it out, and left it bottom up so the floor could dry. When the gang came back from fishing, Beth asked about the tooth. I hoped against hope while my fingers explored the mesh pocket, but the tooth was gone. I walked over to where I thought I'd shaken out the tent, but it really could have been anywhere in an area as big as a half-court in a basketball game. The gravel half-court was littered with tooth-sized bits of white quartz. I felt like I was underwater in a bad dream and still sinking.

"Dad, I'll never forgive you," Charley said.

I wandered around picking up tooth-sized bits, looking for one that could be a tooth if you used your imagination, and showed one to Beth when Charley wasn't looking.

"What do you think?" I whispered.

"Don't even pretend to think you'll get away with it."

We kept searching. Thirty minutes later Beth put her finger to the ground.

"I found it."

Charley ran over and smiled. All was forgiven. Downriver was the Gulkana Bridge, and beyond in Glenallen was a Tastee Freez where we could celebrate the Tooth Fairy coming to the gravel bar with burgers and shakes. As we drifted downriver in the sun, paddles at rest, I thought we had glimpsed what was possible. There would be time to think of more remote trips.

TIKCHIK DELTA

B eth leaned over the top of her paddle, and the canoe rocked like a cradle in the Tikchik River. Charley and Matt were 9 and 6, it'd been two years since the Lower Gulkana, but they still sat side-by-side in the middle. Matt wore a red wool baseball cap sideways on his head. He dug in with his paddle to help. Charley wore a green wool baseball cap tilted up. He gazed at Tikchik Mountain, looming above the birch forest on our left. While we drifted around a bend, I thought of earlier in the trip when Matt and Charley had big smiles while holding up the dorsal fin of a large grayling they'd each landed out of the same hole. Downstream of the bend, the Tikchik's current slowed even more, and the water's surface turned almost placid. The view downriver looked different, so I stood up in the stern. At the other end of a long reach through a tunnel of trees the horizon retreated toward a distant bar.

"We'll be at the lake in 15 minutes."

Beth led us to a grassy spot between alder bushes, where the underwater plants didn't sway or even move. Our 1952 map said there were "ruins" below rock formations bulging out just above us on the hillside, so Charley and Matt scampered through alders and up a bank to the green tundra. By the time we caught up, they were rolling over and over down the slope. We stepped aside and Matt shouted while rolling by.

"LOOK MOM, I'M A LOG!"

We stood on a boulder and looked across the mouth of the river to a spit that spiraled a half-mile out into Tikchik Lake. At the end closest to us, tucked between river and delta, was a broad wrinkled stretch of sand with a grey drift log resting on a high spot in the middle. I pointed at it.

"It's in the breeze," I said.

"You say the same thing every time. It's less exposed over here."

I looked around. There were some flat spots where we could pitch a tent.

"It looks buggy."

She pointed to a soccer field-sized thicket of willows just upriver from the sand bar.

"What about bears?"

"At least we'll be able to see them."

I thought of the morning when Mike Harder was supposed to fly in from Dillingham to pick us up in his twin-engine amphibious Widgeon. I had flown with Harder before on trips into southwest Alaska. He could land his Widgeon in a lake or a river and then crank wheels down so he could drive up onto a beach or gravel bar.

"Harder can taxi right up to that drift log," I said. "Over here, who knows with the submerged rocks?"

Beth relented. Miles across the lake, beyond a cluster of islands, three granite domes rose above a forest floor and black water. They looked like little Half Domes, except the granite was a deep red. Shafts of sunlight lit up the face of the nearest dome, which seemed to glow at us, while a slowly moving rain shower obscured part of the second. We coached the boys back into the canoe and ferried across the river to the sand spit where we set up our North Star dome tent.

During the night, wind ruffled the tent and waves splashed on the beach. At first light, I got out to look. Low clouds obscured the far side of the lake and the granite domes were invisible. Rivulets from whitecaps slapping the shore of our low-lying spit ran up the sand toward us. The closest birch trees, a hundred yards away, bent and swayed. The only possible shelter was the beach log out in the middle. While the boys huddled in their rain gear, Beth and I dragged the tent over and tied it off with thick cord to the log's lee side. The top of the tent was still in the gale, but it wasn't going anywhere. Charley and Matt dove back into their sleeping bags and listened to a story tape about Hank The Cow Dog, self-professed head of ranch security, and his deputy Grover. Something was up in a horse pasture.

"They're going to be hungry soon," Beth said.

"We can't use the stove out here in this wind."

She smiled a knowing smile and ducked back into the tent. I set off across the spit with a camp saw and axe, looking for poles to construct a lean-to for a windbreak we could huddle behind and prepare a meal. A dead spruce, with grey branches propping it up off the ground, lay on the other side of a shallow slough. I waded knee-deep while pushing aside floating sockeye salmon carcasses, limbed the spruce with the axe, and used the camp saw to cut a twelve-foot pole. The only problem was the pole was six inches in diameter on one end, and the tent was two hundred yards away on the other side of the slough. I grabbed the big end of the pole and dragged it through mud, floated it across the slough, and dragged it across the sand. Forty-five minutes for one pole. Then I went to find another. And another. And another. Each time I dropped a pole and sought out another drift log, the next one was farther away. Finally, seven poles lay in a pile next to the tent, and I was soaking wet inside my raingear.

Beth came out. We lashed together two three-legged A-frames and set up a pole between them. The hard parts came next, tying on a large green tarp with the low end facing the gale, and then wrapping a small blue tarp around one corner to keep the wind away from the stove. During a break in the rain, Charley and Matt came out and lay on their stomachs studying spiders hunkered down inside cracks in the sand. By the time the lean-to was erected, we'd used up our rope, runners, cord, bungies, and carabiners. It billowed in the full force of the gale, and looked like a big sheet in full sail on a tall ship.

"Let's play UNO," Charley said.

"Yeah," Matt said in a loud voice.

I set up the camp stove behind the tarp on a spot where I could kneel in the sand and cook. While I was trying to light it, I spotted a brown bear behind a dune on the edge of the spit, close to the willow thicket. When I stood up, it bolted back into the willows. I got the stove started and looked up again. Two brown bears pounced on spawned-out sockeyes in the shallow channel I had floated the first pole across.

"YO BEAR," I shouted.

They shook their heads and broke away from the carcasses, but then ran back. I shouted again. Beth and the boys got out to catch a glimpse of them disappearing around a bend in the lake. When they returned to the UNO game, I pulled my twelve-gauge out of a dry bag, checked the magazine, and leaned it against a spruce pole. In another hour the bears were back, this time a lot closer to our camp. I stuck my head in through the tent door.

"You should see this."

They got out and stood next to me. The bears were on the other side of the tent, maybe fifty yards away, running toward us from the willows and then circling back. Each time they crowded closer. I thought by their size and behavior they were sibling two-year-olds given the boot by mom and didn't yet know what to do. In other words: juvenile delinquents. Instead of pumping a rifled slug into the shotgun's chamber, I pulled out an aerial flare the size of a cigar. They're made for water rescues and shoot a red fire ball a hundred yards into the sky. Sort of like a roman candle except that it sounds like a high-powered rifle. I'd carried them before and thought they'd be good for scaring off bears.

I told Beth and the boys to cover their ears, aimed the flare into the air, and pulled on the string. It ignited with a loud report, and the red ball shot into the air a hundred feet above the delinquents' heads. Instead of running off, they rose on their hind legs and twirled around like tango dancers following the arc of the flare. When the flare descended out of sight, they dropped down on all fours and charged straight toward us.

"Everyone get together," Beth said in a calm voice.

We stood side-by-side and raised our arms. Twenty yards from the tent the siblings veered to our right and galloped in a curve toward the willow thicket, sand flying off their hind legs until their brown rumps disappeared into a sea of green. Beth had her arms around the boys. Nobody said a word.

The gale raged all day and the rest of the night, but the siblings never came back. We played UNO and listened to a story tape where Hank investigated something suspicious about a drainpipe and a rattlesnake bit him on the end of his nose. In the morning I heard a distant rumble and got out of the tent to see a Widgeon heading straight for us under scudding clouds. When we were harnessed in and taxiing out into the lake, I asked Charley what he liked best about the trip.

"Hank and Uno in the tent."

"Yeah," Matt said in a loud voice, "Hank and Uno."

The idea nagged at me all the way back to Dillingham.

SHOWDOWN AT NIMGUN CREEK

Mike Harder cranked down the wheels of his amphibious Widgeon, drove out of Goodnews Lake in southwest Alaska, and spun the plane around on a rocky beach. We climbed out of the rear hatch and Harder started handing out coolers and bags. The pristine waters of the lake beckoned, and Charley asked if he could fish even before all our gear and food were unloaded. He was ten, still wore his hair with a tail, and was reading science fiction, but he had also gotten the taste of a fish on every cast. Matt chimed in. He was seven. He still had a buzz cut and had already proven to be a serious angler. I nodded and searched through the pile of gear for our tube of fiberglass rods. It was only while Harder taxied away that I realized I'd left the tube behind in Dillingham. We did have an Eagle Claw backpacking rod as a backup, but I'd promoted the Goodnews River because of its coho run and fine char and rainbow. The boys didn't like the idea of trading off.

"Dad," Charley said, his brow wrinkled, "it won't be fun."

"What other choice do we have?" I asked.

The boys had grown taller since we first purchased our 18-foot canoe,

too tall for all of us if they sat side-by-side in the middle, so we'd purchased a second canoe sixteen feet in length. Beth and I loaded the 16-footer for her and Charley, and the 18-footer for Matt and me. We shoved off, paddled for an hour toward the lake's outlet, and beached the canoes on the downwind side of a rocky point so we could camp on a crescent pebble beach. Ruins of some wooden buildings were visible a mile down the lake. I walked over after dinner, picked through scattered junk, and found a charred broomstick and a piece of a fiberglass tent pole.

Back at camp, sitting next to a campfire, the boys watched while I used my Swiss army knife and pliers to fabricate a fiberglass rod with a long wooden shaft and eyes made of steel wire wrapped with duct tape. In the following days they spoke of it with disdain as "the homemade rod," and competed for the Eagle Claw, which they called "the good rod." They hadn't yet realized the homemade rod's long handle and stiff tent pole could lob a weighted spoon far beyond what the good rod could do. By the time we arrived at Nimgun Creek, fifty miles downriver from the lake, it was Matt's turn at the good rod.

We pitched our North Star tent just upstream of an alder thicket at the lower end of a long gravel bar. Storms had been coming upriver off the Bering Sea and I wanted the tent to be in the lee of the thicket if it started to blow. The Goodnews River was narrow and shallow in front of the tent, and we had a good view of pyramid peaked Nagyagat Mountain, where afternoon sun splayed out between cloud shadows on yellowing tundra. A large black boulder sat half in the water on the opposite bank, not twenty yards away. The boys skipped rocks across trying to hit it. There were a lot of good, flat, smooth stones for the job, so I joined them.

It must be a glacial erratic.

I had read that the topography of the Goodnews valley formed when a volcano erupted under a glacier and lava spread out beneath a thick platter of shifting ice. That explained the horizontal layers of smooth black basalt we'd seen in steep bluffs and outcroppings while coming downriver. I imagined the glacier shearing off some basalt at an outcropping and turning it over and over again on the way to depositing the boulder we were skipping rocks at across the river. Beth came over and found a nice flat one.

"I think we should take a harbor day," she said.

She tossed the rock and it skipped four times. "Harbor day" is a term leftover from her years on commercial salmon boats. I knew what she meant. It had been a wet trip so far and we couldn't count on good weather ahead. She wanted us to stay long enough to dry sleeping bags and other gear, and wash dirty clothes in a plastic tub and dry them in the sun. I eyed upriver to the mouth of Nimgun Creek, where the Goodnews pooled deep and wide before narrowing into a fast race. About as ideal a spot to fish as there could be.

"Why not?"

We set up a folding table and Beth started prepping food under a tan parawing tarp. Charley read Ender's Game in a camp chair while Matt and I walked upriver. He carried the good rod and I carried the homemade one. At the pool, he cast with the good rod, but the spoon only went half way across, and he reeled in without a strike.

"Here, try this one."

He grabbed the broomstick end of the homemade rod with both hands, flung a silver and pink spoon nearly to the opposite shore, and turned the crank on the spinning reel. He turned three times and paused, three times and paused. The tent pole bent over, the drag screamed, and line stripped out through the eyes made of steel wire and duct tape.

"FISH ON," he shouted.

A brawny coho salmon leaped clear out of the water, shaking its head and flapping its tail like it was climbing a waterfall. Then it surged ahead while leaping one, two, three, four, five more times, each time clearing the pool's surface, and ran downriver trying to get into the fast race. Matt kept the tip up and dragged it to the beach. I grabbed it by its gills, banged its head with a rock, and laid it in Matt's arms.

"Take it to mom."

He headed back down the bar with a big smile on his face, holding the fish high against his chest with both arms, stumbling over rocks he couldn't see.

"LOOK MOM," he shrieked.

Beth filleted the salmon and we ate most of it for dinner. In the morning I woke early. Fog smothered the river bar. I shook Charley awake and asked him if he wanted to fish the morning bite. He remembered me asking him the same question on another morning on a different river. Then, he shook his head, so I took Matt, who landed two fat grayling in five minutes and never let Charley forget it. This time Charley jumped out of his sleeping bag. He'd heard Matt's story about the coho and selected the homemade rod. As we walked upriver, the camp disappeared into the fog behind us, and our voices echoed.

At the pool, Charley picked out a red and gold spinner and used both hands to cast it to the far side of the pool. As soon as he started to reel in a large arctic char with a bullet shaped head and a reddish orange belly erupted from the pool and surged downriver with its dorsal fin out of the water. It startled Charley, and in the instant he hesitated I thought the char was going to slip into the fast race where it could break the line, but Charley got his tip up and stopped the run. Soon, it was flopping and splashing right in front of us. Charley stepped in over the top of his rubber boots and grabbed it behind the head. I walked out and took the fish so he could cast again. On his second cast, the tent pole bent double and another bright bellied char surfaced, rolling over and over. That char was bigger than the first. It was bigger than any char I had ever caught. I coaxed Charley to stand by the canoe, holding one in each hand, while I took a photo. His smile looked twisted, one end up, the other down, like he wasn't sure what he had done.

In late afternoon, things were quiet while clothes dried on a line and I searched for driftwood. Matt put down his book, picked up the homemade rod, and walked upriver toward the confluence. He cast into the race below the pool. Beth shot me a glance.

"I've got my eye on him," I said.

I bent over to gather an armful of willows. When I looked up, a chocolate colored brown bear stood on top of a grassy cut bank across the river. It was upstream from where Matt fished, but it was hard from our position to see how close it really was.

"MATT," Beth shouted.

Matt had already seen the bear, but he cast again and looked over his shoulder at Beth.

"Mom," he pleaded, "can't I just have ten more casts?"

The bear disappeared behind some leafy willows and then came back into view, twenty yards closer to Matt. He looked up at the bear, glanced at us over his shoulder, and cast again.

"COME THIS WAY," Beth shouted.

She ran toward Matt, pulled him away from the water's edge, put her arm around his shoulder, and ushered him toward our camp, turning her head to look back. During this whole time the bear kept moving downriver. It didn't move fast, but it didn't plod either.

Deliberate.

I reached for my stainless steel twelve-gauge shotgun and unfolded the fiberglass stock so it was a full-length shoulder weapon. By the time I looked up, the bear was standing across the river from where Matt had been fishing. It turned our direction with ears alert. They looked small against a big head. That's when I realized how big the bear really was. And, it was a boar. I thought it wasn't a good sign.

Big old boar out here on the tundra?

We stood side-by-side next to the tent waving our arms.

"YO BEAR, YO BEAR," we shouted.

When it kept moving, I pumped a rifled slug into the chamber of the shotgun. The bear slowed down and ambled along the top of the bank before it stopped directly across the river. It reached out with an enormous paw to step down the bank, and I brought the shotgun to my shoulder. It mounted the black boulder, stood there on all fours like a statue, and looked straight at us. Another bad sign. I pushed the safety off, squinted down the barrel to locate the sight, and tightened my index finger on the trigger.

What's it going to be?

The bear stiffened on its haunches like it was going to pounce.

"Get behind me."

The bear dove head first into the river and stood up on its hind legs with a wriggling coho in its jaws and orange salmon eggs squirting out of its mouth. It tossed its head, dropped down on all fours, shook the water off its back, and splashed downriver with the salmon still twitching. The alder bushes blocked our view. I rushed to glimpse where it was going, grasping the twelve-gauge, hoping that it was done with us, that it had made its point, but when I pushed through the alder it had disappeared. I walked back glancing over my shoulder. It was too late to vacate the gravel bar. We'd have to spend the night, and I knew I wasn't going to get a lot of sleep.

RETURN TO BEAVER CREEK

Ten-year-old Matt tugged on his rod and looked over his shoulder at me with a "what can I do about it?" look. His spinner was caught on a waterlogged stick rising up from the bottom. He had gotten many hooks dislodged on his own, but this one was in a spot over his head. We were camped on a sandy peninsula inside a horseshoe bend on the upper stretch of Beaver Creek in Interior Alaska. Grayling darted about in pools all around us.

Charley was thirteen and had elected to solo in a twelve-foot inflatable canoe. He sat in a camp chair next to our friends John and Sonia, his face deep into a fantasy book about a girl on a planet in a different solar system going on a quest. I pointed toward Charley's canoe and Matt got a big grin on his face. He grabbed a paddle, tossed in his rod, and shoved the canoe into the water with a flourish. Once in the current, he alternated between frenzied paddling, grabbing the rod, and trying to get his hands on the stick with the spinner. His problem was he had to keep switching hands.

"USE A J-STROKE," I shouted.

He did, stroking alongside the gunwale and then pushing the flat of his paddle blade out to correct his direction, and managed to coax the canoe alongside the stick so he could plunge a hand into the tea colored water.

"ALRIGHT!"

It was our family's return to Beaver Creek, a long pristine river north of Fairbanks. Five years earlier, the boys were five and eight, and I thought they were ready for their first real bush river trip. I proposed we spend ten days paddling the middle stretch of Beaver Creek, where it winds for over a hundred miles through the jagged White Mountains, and called a Fairbanks friend who had paddled it in a canoe. Dave was in his sixties but his mustache and hair were still brown. He brought maps to the café where we had lunch and handed me handwritten notes from three different trips. I asked him if the middle stretch was a good venue for a family trip. He nodded.

"I've always sought out new rivers," I said, "but you've paddled the same stretch of Beaver Creek three times."

He got a mischievous grin on his face.

"Would you choose to make love to a beautiful woman only once?"

When I told Beth what Dave had said, she was onboard. It was a warm day and the boys wore tie-dyed shirts when we stood on the tarmac in Fairbanks. Charley and I flew out first in a white Cessna 185 with half our food and gear. The pilot landed on a short flat spot alongside a fast channel the color of weak tea. Northward, grey limestone towers gleamed above a dark green spruce forest. Beth and Matt flew in two hours later with the rest of the food and gear. As Beth and I assembled and packed the 18-foot canoe, the boys rigged their spinning rods and started pulling out grayling. They cleaned them on rocks with a Swiss Army knife. Charley studied the scales.

"Sometimes they change colors."

"That's called iridescent," Beth said. "Turn them in the light."

We were a day upriver from the Big Bend on Beaver Creek, a hundred and eighty-degree loop around the western perimeter of the White Mountains. The next morning we drifted over deep pools along low cut banks with blueberry bushes and leaning spruce trees. As we passed by a low hill, I spotted something peeking out between spruce trees I thought could be a roofline, but then we were by it, and I put it out of my mind. Along the Big Bend, we stared up at rugged limestone towers and camped on a huge gravel bar beneath a long mountain ridge. Below the ridge were near vertical grey limestone walls and below the walls steep slopes dropped all the way to the river, here and there punctuated by limestone towers and outcroppings, some of which looked a little like Stonehenge.

I've learned there is something different about boreal escarpments beneath natural limestone fortifications and that was true of the slopes above us. There weren't any alder or willow thickets or dense patches of scrub birch. Instead, green spruce spread out like sentries across lush tundra meadows populated with blueberry bushes and wildflowers. The dark green trees in the lighter green meadows mixed with the grey and near white towers and walls into what felt like a natural cathedral. We pitched our North Star tent on a sandy spot with a good view and set up a blue tarp over the kitchen. I cut branches from dead spruce left behind during a spring flood and built a fire. Charley kept looking up at the slopes and walls and spires.

"Does this place have a name?" he asked.

"It doesn't have one on the map," I replied.

"I'm going to call it Symmetrical Mountain," he announced.

After dinner, Charley said he wanted to climb Symmetrical Mountain. I knew imaginative ideas often took hold of Charley's mind. The previous year, he'd imagined the view from a bench across a river valley in the Wrangell Mountains, and decided on a whim to sprint up a forested slope so fast I had trouble catching up with him. It was his way of connecting with the wilderness. But there, beneath Symmetrical Mountain at the end of a long day, I was tired and the idea of climbing up steep slopes to pursue Charley's imagination did not appeal.

"What, now?"

"Yes."

"It's too steep, Charley, and it is a lot farther up there than it looks."

Beth took me aside.

"He's serious," she said in a quiet voice. "Don't squash him."

I walked over to Charley.

"How about we go in the morning," I said, "that way we'll have lots of time."

His brow furled and he looked down.

"Drat."

The next day was sunny. Beth and Matt picked blueberries in meadows between evenly spaced spruce trees. When Charley and I approached, Beth pointed out purple and white Lady Slipper orchids brightening the berry patch. We left them and zigzagged up to a rocky platform overlooking a limestone tower shaped like a castle turret. Alone on top of the turret, a tall spruce tree stood surrounded by bright green moss campion cushions blooming with pinkish flowers.

"Let's call it Sentinel Rock," I said. "Think of the spruce tree as a guard watching over our camp."

Charley smiled and nodded. A whistle came from above, and we looked up.

"What's that?" he asked.

I pointed to a landslide below the limestone wall, where boulders spread out down the tundra-covered slope.

"See that dark spot on the boulder right at the bottom?"

"Yeah."

"It's an arctic ground squirrel standing up and looking at us. It whistles to alert others."

"I want to go up and see them," he said.

I started to protest but thought of the night before. We put on wind gear and climbed higher, switching back and forth up steep meadows and around other towers toward the wall. After nearly an hour it dawned on me that the ground squirrels were moving up through the boulders in the landslide at the same pace.

"We won't catch up with them, Charley."

"Maybe they'll stop."

"I don't think so. We should go down and find your mom and Matt."

"Drat."

Charley was quiet on the way down. That evening, I watched while he stared up at Sentinel Rock, his face alive with emotion. I wanted to say "let's go back up tomorrow, we can get above the ground squirrels," but I thought of our pledge to meet our pilot on a gravel bar a hundred miles downriver. I let my logistical mind take over, *we'd have to rush*, I thought, and said nothing to Charley. It's a decision I'll always regret.

We broke camp the next morning and spent another week on the river as it cut through the White Mountains toward the Yukon Flats. All the way downriver I worried I'd stifled my oldest son's imagination where I wanted it most, in the outdoors. With the hills behind us and the flats in front of us, we found the right gravel bar by spotting a piece of blue surveyor's tape tied to a willow branch. By then I knew we had to go back.

***

When we returned five years later, we were with friends, and our plan was to paddle the upper stretch of Beaver Creek from its headwaters to a takeout just downriver from the Big Bend. We had four canoes. Our friend John was with eleven-year-old Joe in one. Matt and I were in ours. Beth and Sonja in a third. Charley in his twelve-foot inflatable. Five days after putting in, we arrived at the sandy peninsula where Matt used Charley's canoe to retrieve his fishing lure.

Charley was thirteen, artistic, and still read lots of science fiction. He was a natural in the outdoors but not always enthusiastic about getting anywhere because he got very focused on one thing. One porcupine. One fish. One fireweed. I thought then Matt would become an outdoorsman. He was ten and reading *Hatchet*, a novel about a boy surviving in the wilderness on his own.

It was only two days to the takeout below the Big Bend. I thought about Sentinel Rock and Symmetrical Mountain. I wanted to be back there with Charley, to let him go wherever he wanted to go, to let his imagination run free. Rain clouds piled in from the south the next morning. A few miles downriver, the temperature dropped, wind gusted, and heavy rain started. It felt like a coastal storm. We didn't have the right clothes for the temperature and everyone was cold. John went on ahead with Joe so they could stop every hour or so to build a fire of dead spruce branches broken off standing trees. When the rest of us arrived, they'd have a blue tarp spread out for us to stand under. By late afternoon we shivered under the tarp during a downpour wondering what to do. I imagined a freak show where our sleeping bags got soaked before we could get them out of their dry bags and into tents that were already soaked, but then a vague memory of a roofline pushed into my mind. I pulled out a USGS topographic map last updated in 1952. A tiny black square close to the blue line of Beaver Creek was just a few bends downriver from where we stood. Those squares were cabins on those old maps. I beckoned Beth and John and Sonia around me and pointed to the square.

"I may have seen the roofline on our trip five years ago," I said. "Who knows whether it's still standing."

We agreed to gamble rather than accept the certainty of a wet and cold night on that bar. All the way downriver I prayed for something.

Just a roof, even if there isn't a door or windows.

When the river swung up against a hill, I stood up in our canoe to scan the slopes and spotted something in the spruce trees that looked out of place. We tied up to willows on a muddy bank and walked along the top until we saw a trail. I raced the boys uphill to the front of a log cabin. It had a roof. And windows. I shoved open a homemade door. A wooden table and bunks and a wood stove were inside. On top of the stove sat a box of Diamond matches. Inside the stove split kindling rested on wadded up newspaper. I struck a match. The paper smoked, then lit, and the kindling started to crackle. The boys cheered.

In the morning the river had risen three feet and our canoes strained against their lines. We lingered, hoping for the water to drop, but we had to meet the air taxi in two days and launched anyway in early afternoon. The current was fast and the river spilled over muddy banks and broke across bars littered with root systems that were dry the day before. Charley paddled behind Matt and me.

"STAY CLOSE," I shouted.

We came to a spot where the channel split around a logjam stacked up on the end of a muddy island. I couldn't see right, and worried a hidden sweeper could be all the way across that channel. More water seemed to go left, so that's the way we went. I looked back over my shoulder and Charley wasn't there. Had he gone right?

"Get ready Matt, we're going to drive the bow onto the beach."

We stroked for the shore of the island. When the bow slid up onto mud and then silt, the stern swung around in the current, but Matt was ready and hopped out, grabbed the bowline, and held the canoe. I dropped my paddle and sprinted across the island.

"CHARLEY. CHARLEY."

When I reached the opposite shore, all I found was the channel slipping by. I raced upriver to get a look around a jumble of trees.

"CHARLEY. CHARLEY."

A root system hung up in the current but there was no sign. I raced back downriver toward the other end of the island, but got held up by trees stacked along the shore.

"CHARLEY."

Nothing. I ran back to Matt standing by our canoe.

"Get in and let's go."

We dug deep in unison with our paddles. When we passed the downriver end of the island, the brown bow of Charley's canoe surged out from the other channel.

"Where were you?"

He shrugged.

"I got stuck along the shore."

I held my tongue. I was just grateful he was safe. The day warmed as we paddled around the Big Bend. The ridge above the river with limestone towers and walls seemed only oddly familiar. When we arrived at a huge gravel bar I looked up again, and realized we were below Symmetrical Mountain, but a wildfire had ravaged the mountainside. That evening Beth sat on her knees cooking grayling over a fire while Charley read the book about the girl on a different world. I nudged his foot and pointed upward.

"Do you remember this place?"

He looked up. The green tundra slope with blueberry bushes and orchids we had zigzagged up was a sooty grey with big orange spots. Some spruce still stood but were scorched and spindly, and the solitary spruce on top of Sentinel Rock had burned and pitched down the face into a charred heap at the bottom.

"What do you call it?" he asked.

"Symmetrical Mountain. Do you remember the ground squirrels?"

"Sort of."

I looked downriver to where Beaver Creek disappeared around a bend. Uprooted trees from the flood littered the next gravel bar. I wondered why I thought we could ever go home again.

THE CONGRESSMAN

D ave disappeared into a willow thicket with Frankie. They had just met, Frankie was unsteady on his feet, and it was still morning. We were in the Interior Alaska village of McGrath, packing for a river trip next to a boat landing on the Kuskokwim River. Dave had a scraggly beard, was tall and barrel chested, and had an old man's gut. He lived with a grey haired Inupiaq girlfriend in a plywood house in Spenard where he sold small bags of weed. Years before, when Reagan was president, he ran against Don Young for Alaska's sole congressional seat. Young had been in office forever even then, and Dave denounced Reagan as a war criminal on the campaign trail, but he still received almost forty percent of the vote. After that he was always the Congressman. Whenever I went to his house, I would push open his door and shout "I NEED AN APPROPRIATION."

We had spent the morning hauling gear from the McGrath airport, and commandeered a picnic table across a gravel street from the boat landing. Frankie emerged from nearby B. J's Café and walked over. He was a short Athabascan man with long black hair and a dark ball cap cocked on his head. He wore a tattered black nylon jacket and greasy black jeans. Dave joked around with Frankie while I worked. I had designated Dave as our ambassador with McGrath locals so I could keep my head down while getting the collapsible canoe assembled and loaded. After they yucked it up a bit, Frankie came over to watch me pound the last aluminum ribs into place on the canoe.

"Where you going?"

"Stony River."

"Why so early to Stony?"

It wasn't a bad question. It was mid-May in Interior Alaska, none of the birch or cottonwood or alder had leafed out, and pans of ice floated by in the Kuskokwim's muddy current. I didn't tell Frankie going early was my idea. That I sought out May trips on big rivers. That I wanted to be on the river right after breakup, taking my time, "hoboing it downriver" one friend called it, while everything was fresh, animals were moving about, and there were no footprints on the gravel bars. I thought he probably hadn't considered those things, so instead I put on a worried look and slapped my forehead.

"It's early?"

He sucked air through the hole where his two front teeth used to be and walked off down a trail into the willow thicket. He came back a half-hour later weaving around. I knew Dave had weed in his jeans pocket when he followed Frankie back into the thicket. I thought it wasn't a good sign.

"CONGRESSMAN," I shouted, "KEEP YOUR HEAD."

Dave and I had never done a trip together. I'd called Fish and Game in McGrath and learned the ice in the Kuskokwim had "gone out" and the left-over shore ice was melting. My river-running buddies afflicted with "Channel Fever" usually turned their noses up at the thought of paddling a big muddy river, even if their aspirations were still frozen solid. It was no different then, so I was planning a solo trip when I went to visit Dave in his house surrounded by old cars, vacuum cleaners, refrigerators and other surplus sale items he had collected. I pushed his door open and followed a trail through waist high piles of newspapers, many still in their plastic wrappers, to a small table where he sat reading. Resting on the table was a pipe made from the tip of a walrus tusk. I admired it while saying I was going to paddle from McGrath to Stony River. He said he had always wanted to see that part of the country and asked who was going with me.

"Going solo, Dave."

He grimaced.

"Du-ugh, do-on't do that."

Dave had a funny way of dragging out his vowels and I laughed. But then, he volunteered to go along if it meant I didn't go alone. I told him I would think it over. It wasn't that I wanted company. I relished the idea of another solo trip. But I liked Dave. He had a cackling laugh accompanied by occasional snorting that always cracked me up. I knew he had spent time in bush Alaska and could probably sleep under a tarp anywhere, but he had never been on a long river trip through wild country. I asked Beth, who had been with me on many trips, knew how focused I could be on logistics, and played the ambassador role when it was just the two of us. She worried about me when I was out there alone.

"If he can keep up, you're better off to have someone to talk to," she said.

I went back to Dave's house.

"Can you paddle all day?"

"I'm sure I can."

I said we would take our collapsible 18-foot Allypak canoe. That meant we could carry a cooler, roll up table, and camp chairs. A week later Dave disappeared down the trail with Frankie. When he returned, I asked him about Frankie's whereabouts and he pointed toward the café. There, next to a fire pit, Frankie lay face down in the yellow grass of early spring with his forehead resting on his arms.

Other locals showed up. They were used to seeing beamy aluminum or plywood riverboats with big outboard motors hanging off the transoms. One wondered out loud how long it would take to get to Stony, over a hundred miles downriver. He snorted and raised his eyebrows when I said the river was low and the wind was blowing upriver, so it could take ten days. Another questioned whether the canoe's synthetic rubber hull would hold up against ice. He wrinkled his forehead when I said we could avoid the floes and they should be gone in a couple more days anyway. He said we would have trouble in the "Devil's Elbow." I had seen the Devil's Elbow on my maps. It was sixty miles downriver where the river squeezed between some hills to form a long "S." I asked him if he had ever been there in a small boat. He said "no," but friends of his had and they told him about "big swirls."

We loaded the canoe. I told Dave to sit in the lawn chair in the bow. It was his first time in the canoe and I wanted to see how he handled it. I settled onto a cooler in the stern and swiveled my hips from one side to another to make the canoe rock. Dave gripped the gunwales on each side with both hands like he was on a roller coaster.

"WHOO-AAA."

"Dave, this is what it feels like. It's going to rock but it won't turn over."

He groaned. The two locals looked down from the top of the bank.

"How could anyone think they'll make it to Stony in that?" one asked.

Two hours later we were camped on a long gravel bar five miles downriver from McGrath. Even though we could still hear planes taking off from the airport, red-crowned sandhill cranes strutted around the upstream end of the bar, and white fronted geese barked "kla-ha" from the downstream end. We sat for a long time around a driftwood fire, listening to KSKO in McGrath on Dave's transistor radio. That night the temperatures fell below freezing. In the morning heavy frost coated the tent when Dave got out to take a leak.

"DU-UGH!"

I climbed out and walked over to Dave. He pointed at the tip of a mammoth tusk sticking out of the gravel. A tiny bit of frost covered the very top. It turned out to be eight inches long, and was burnished by the river turning it over and over again in the sand and gravel and silt. It is impossible to travel rivers in Alaska without finding feathers, semi-precious rocks, old tools, and remains of ancient creatures, particularly right after the spring floods. I usually leave stuff, but I knew immediately Dave would want to keep the ivory. So, I decided to tell him a story about a guy who'd been on a canoe trip in Alaska and found the skull of a Pleistocene American Lion partially buried in the gravel, complete with big incisors. After he returned, he somehow ended up on CNN with the skull. I told Dave I imagined a banner scrolling across the bottom of the screen: SABER TOOTHED CAT. It took only a week for federal agents to knock on his door. The skull belonged to the federal government they said, and demanded it back. The river he had been on coursed through a checkerboard of state and federal land, so he was able to negotiate a solution where he donated it to a natural history museum. When I finished the story, Dave looked at me with desperation in his eyes.

"Du-ugh."

"Just don't get on CNN."

We waited until the frost melted, and shoved off into a slow river with ice pans drifting in the current. The pans made gurgling sounds when they turned over. Sometimes they flashed white and made me think a fish had rolled. The river meandered back and forth in long swoops and a chilly wind blew in our faces, slicing right through bare trees. Over the next three days we struggled with upriver winds, forcing us to paddle long hours. At one camp the canoe was unloaded and turned upside down when Dave mumbled something about his "ticker." I walked over in front of him and asked what he meant. He said he had a pacemaker and thought his heart might not be beating rhythmically.

"What? Why didn't I know about that?"

He got a sheepish look and shrugged.

"Dave," I said, my voice rising, "there is no easy way for us to get you out of here if you're in trouble."

He looked down at his feet. I grabbed the canoe, flipped it over, and pointed at it. It looked like a coffin without the lid.

"ALL I CAN DO IS LAY YOU OUT AND GO DOWNRIV-ER," I shouted.

"I'll make it," he said.

We struggled again the next day. I told Dave to take it easy but he insisted on paddling. That night, we camped on a mostly barren island with some sandy spots big enough for a tent and a kitchen area. Dave and I sat in our camp chairs while he drank a can of Pabst Blue Ribbon and I sipped on a cup of box chardonnay. Orange light streaked the western sky. Across a narrow channel from our island, a large grizzly with a blond head and chocolate ears stepped out of a dense thicket. Dave whispered.

"Will it figure out we're here?"

I walked slowly to the canoe where my .44 magnum Smith & Wesson was stowed in a dry bag.

"Du-ugh."

He motioned across the channel. Three brown cubs spilled out of the thicket and scrambled after the sow. She rolled over in dead yellow grass on the riverbank. The cubs piled on top to suckle at her teats. She pushed her head and shoulders up with her front legs behind her. We watched with binoculars while the cubs jockeyed for position and her head swayed back and forth. At one point she seemed to look right at us, but then she turned her head away. Finally, she appeared satisfied, laid her head back, and rested. The cubs were hard at it, pulling away and then diving back on in a frantic competition. I felt like a voyeur and finally looked away and handed the binoculars back to Dave. After another twenty minutes, the cubs ran to a grassy spot and started rough housing. The sow rose slowly and moved away. By then, the cubs were taking turns pouncing on a tuft of dead yellow grass, first one, then another. When the sow got to the edge of a pussy willow thicket, she looked back and grunted. The cubs scampered after her and they disappeared.

We awoke in the morning to clear skies and downriver winds, and Dave said he was feeling better. I angled the bow so the broad side of the canoe was like a sail, and when the wind caught it we sped along so fast we sent out a bow wave. The only sound was the wind murmuring in our ears and the creak of the canoe. The muddy river looked as big as the blue sky above, and the land was a mere sliver of green on a distant horizon. When the current swept us along the shore, we saw peregrine falcons in cottonwood aeries. Without any leaf cover, the nests were exposed and down covered chicks stared at us. Adults screeched, fluffed up their leg feathers, and flew steeply banked circles over our heads with rapidly flapping wings.

On the sixth day, we entered a series of bends where the river narrowed between hills and the current speeded up. We came to a sharp bend to the left. It was the beginning of the "Devil's Elbow" the local boys had referred to back in McGrath. Ever since Dave heard about the "big swirls" he'd acted superstitious about the name Devil's Elbow. In the days before we got to that part of the river, he refused to use the word "Devil" at all, instead referring to the rapid as "Double Elbow." When we arrived at the bluff where the river broke to the left, I scouted from the beach and concluded we could easily run it.

"Can't we just line the canoe along the shore?" Dave asked.

It was late in the day, and lining meant pushing and dragging the canoe along the river's edge. That would take time. At one spot we would have to unload and carry some of the cargo.

"It's just too much work Dave. We can run it right down the middle."

He stiffened, but climbed back in the canoe. We paddled quietly up to the edge of a drop where a tongue of water stretched out downstream. The current pulled the bow over the lip and down the fall line and we were through the rapid in seconds. Dave pumped his fist. At camp, he referred to the stretch we had just run as "Devil's Canyon." Devil's Canyon is a gorge on the Susitna River in central Alaska with some of the biggest whitewater in North America.

"What, it was Double Elbow before and it's Devil's Canyon after?" I teased.

He pumped his fist again.

"WE MADE IT THROUGH," he shouted.

On the afternoon of the ninth day, we drifted down to a boat landing with riverboats pulled up on a gravel beach. It was hot, our first truly hot day, and we were happy to discover that the end of the Stony River landing strip was only a short carry away. Villagers dropped by to watch while we unloaded and dismantled the canoe. I hauled a load up to the landing strip. When I returned, Dave stood in a circle with two young Athabascan men, holding a fresh sheefish he had traded for some cheese and red beans. They were all laughing. I edged in and asked how long it took a boat to go upriver to McGrath.

"Five hours," one claimed.

"You must be kidding," I said.

He took us to see his homemade plywood boat. It was no longer than our canoe, with just room enough for one person to sit behind a windscreen to operate the steering wheel, and a well in front for gear and fuel. A hundred and fifty horse outboard motor hung on the back. He patted its side and gave a big toothy grin.

"Fastest boat on the river."

Dave pulled out a disposable camera and asked me to take a picture of him with his arm around the guy's shoulder. The mail plane came and we loaded our gear on board. Dave died of a stroke a few years later. It seemed like all of Anchorage was at his memorial service. Until the end, whenever I stopped by to say hello, he pulled out the polished tip of the mammoth tusk and the picture of him with the guy who had the fastest boat on the river, and replayed the time we ran Devil's Canyon in a canoe. ●

TOE STORY

The floats on Dave Doyon's red De Havilland Beaver chafed against his dock. It was mid-May in southern Southeast Alaska, and light wind ruffled dark water beneath a cloudy sky. Dave had a big round face and a ready smile. He wore jeans and a navy blue fleece jacket with a logo that read Misty Fjords Air. My friend John and I were dressed for full conditions: Grunden bibs and tops, wool hats and gloves, and red XTRATUF boots. We ran through our mental checklists while Dave walked up his ramp to check on the weather. He came back with the news it was blowing on the outer coast of Prince of Wales Island. He said he could put us down in a bay at the site of an old cannery, but the forecast for the evening was a full-blown gale.

"Do you want to wait?"

There was no hint of a smile when he asked the question. I looked at John, an old friend who grew up in Ketchikan. We'd never been on a sea kayak trip together but we had spent plenty of time running rivers. His usually expressive dark eyes deferred to me. I looked at Dave.

"We'd rather go now, so we're there when the storm clears."

He nodded. We climbed into the Beaver. The big radial engine roared to life, we taxied out into Tongass Narrows, and took off south from Ketchikan. Prince of Wales Island is a hundred and thirty five miles long north to south, and has the most coastline in Southeast Alaska. We were headed across the island to the South Prince of Wales Wilderness. Soon we were flying along the island's mountainous east coast. The angled deck of a cargo ship that foundered a half century ago was our cue to turn west. The plane bounced around in the pass and I grabbed a handhold, as if that would hold me up if we went down.

Dave circled in a steep bank above the old cannery site. A gust caught the left wing tip and blew the Beaver over on its side. It dropped like a runaway elevator, my shoulder harness dug in, and the engine quit. I looked straight out the window and all I could see was beach. Dave reached up to the dash, restarted the engine, and turned toward a line of rotted pilings without saying a word. I looked back at John. His dark eyes were on fire and looked as big as the giant black mussels we found in Southeast tide pools.

Dave landed close to the wooden pilings sticking up like sentries. Rain fell in sheets and splattered the windshield. He stayed at the controls with the engine running while John and I tossed gear onto a rocky beach. We wrapped ourselves inside a tarp and spray washed over our backs when Dave took off. John grabbed a kayak bag and started down the beach toward a small peninsula with a promise of shelter.

We squeezed our tent under branches and between roots of several large hemlock trees. John's purple coated-nylon tarp was twenty by twenty-four, and we rigged it in higher branches so it was over the tent and there was still plenty of room under it to store the rest of our gear. The gale was blowing the hardest when I crawled out to pee in the middle of the night. My left leg cramped before I could stand up. I hopped off balance on my right leg and kicked out to straighten my left. My toes jammed into something hard and I felt a burning sensation. During the night, throbbing pains woke me. At morning light, I unzipped my sleeping bag and looked at my left foot.

Blood soaked the front half of my sock. Pain surged when I pulled it off. The nail of my big toe was detached and dangled from a thread of flesh. I crawled out again, saw a mark in a hemlock root where my toe had hit it, and hopped down to the beach to fill a plastic tub with seawater. When I stepped in, the nail slipped around on the end of the flesh like a translucent fishing lure. John brought me a camp chair and I soaked my foot for a while. After drying it with my bandanna, I placed the toenail back on top of the mangled toe and looked up at John.

"I need some duct tape."

He handed me a new roll.

"John, next time Dave Doyon asks if we want to wait, we should take him up on it."

He laughed. That evening, when I unwrapped the duct tape bandage and stuck my foot in seawater again, the toe was wrinkled and had turned as white as a midsummer cloud. I thought the flesh was dying and imagined a surgeon squinting at it.

"It's all I know to do," I said.

"Maybe we should radio Dave."

"John, I'm not getting medevaced over a fucking broken toe. I'd never live it down."

He laughed again and pulled out a steel flask of single malt scotch.

"Maybe a little pain killer will help."

It was the first time I had ever sipped scotch. I liked its smoky taste and how it burned all the way down to my stomach.

When we headed south, John was almost always out in front. His outdoor buddies nicknamed him "The Norwegian" because his parents were from Norway, but it could just have easily been because he always pushed ahead like you'd imagine a Viking. The farther south we went toward the Barrier Islands, where the southwest coast of Prince of Wales turns east toward Cape Chacon, the more the wind blew. At low tide late in the afternoon, trees swayed in the wind along a rocky coastline while we looked for a place to camp. John spotted an entrance almost hidden in folds of green kelp draping like curtains off giant boulders and turned toward shore. Ahead, limbs of Sitka spruce and Western hemlock stretched toward us over the placid black water of a lagoon. John paddled in quietly while I kibitzed from behind that we couldn't possibly find a place in that jungle to set up our tent. The lagoon was bigger than it looked at the entrance and wrapped around a peninsula. At its end a rocky beach curled in front of a grove of old growth red cedar. The trees were five or six feet in diameter, twenty feet apart, and the ground between them was littered with dead limbs. We cleared a spot big enough for a tent and broke the limbs into firewood. The spruce and hemlock on the opposite side of the lagoon leaned toward us, but the water was quiet at our beach. I put both hands on a cedar and felt it tremble.

In the early evening, I decided to walk back out of the lagoon to get a better look at the weather. When I arrived at the entrance, a cove stretching out to my right was in the lee of the peninsula. A tree-covered island lay offshore, and the inside waters were calm. A kingfisher dove for minnows and flapped back up to the limb of a hemlock. My mind focused on our plan to head offshore to the Barrier Islands even though the wind was blowing with more ferocity. The idea was to paddle to the outer island with its wind stunted trees where there would be nothing beyond except the North Pacific Ocean. I thought of the time Beth and I were trying to find a way in through breakers crashing against rock walls off the coast of Chichagof Island, and how quickly I had felt panic when my kayak surfed down the backside of a wave. I turned my bow into the wind, pointed away from the direction we should be going, and shouted to Beth I was going to wait there until the waves settled down. She paddled alongside, said it was time to go in with a calm voice, and led me through the breakers.

I came out of my thoughts when I heard an orca breathe and saw its fin break the surface of the placid waters inside the island. I realized I'd lost track of time. Darkness approached and I thought I could cut directly across the peninsula to camp. Before long I was picking my way around downed cedar trees six and seven feet in diameter. Standing giants towered eighty feet and blocked out much of the remaining light. I came to a spot where I couldn't go around, so I climbed up the side of a downed cedar, pulling on the tips of my fingers and pushing on the toes of my rubber boots against the uneven bark. I had good footing on top, but pain racked my left foot. Deadfall cedars were strewn all about, like pick-up sticks, only the sticks were as big around as streetcars. I walked down the trunk to another tree and climbed up on it, but it was covered with a slippery moss, so I retreated and jumped to a different one. At the end of that one I stepped on another that hung out over a bank. I down climbed it, facing the trunk with hands spread, digging in again with the toes of my rubber boots, and crawled under. Dead branches camouflaged by darkness slapped my face. My foot burned, I couldn't see, and I wasn't sure which way to go. I limped forward with both hands outstretched until I smelled smoke from a cedar fire. John was feeding deadfall limbs to it when I appeared out of the darkness. Yellow light reflected in his eyes.

"I was beginning to wonder if I should send out a search party."

"John, do you have any more of that pain killer?"

He handed me the flask. I took a sip and carried the flask to the rocky beach where I pulled off my boot and soaked my mangled toe in the lagoon. It was high tide and just enough light was left in the sky for a wall of trees to reflect on the water. My left foot throbbed. I took another sip. The burning taste of peat lingered in my throat while the sweetness of rotting kelp mixed with the pungent smell of burning cedar.

"You going to bogart that flask?" John asked.

I stirred my foot around in the lagoon.

"Just one more."

We had to make our first crossing the next day and thoughts of whitecaps and windward shores lay heavy on my mind.

GET BACK NUSHAGAK

"Dad, I don't see a good place to camp over here."

I turned from fiddling with the pump on our two-burner Coleman stove and looked at Charley. He was twenty-three then, and at six-foot-six stood five inches taller than me. Skinny. Curly brown hair sticking out from under the hood of a blue-grey sweatshirt I'd loaned him. Dark glasses. Rain pants. Rubber boots. Lips pursed.

"Sure there is," I said. "Other side of that spruce log is a spot big enough for your tent."

He glanced in the direction of the silvered log, complete with tangled root system as big as a car, ripped out of the riverbank during a spring flood and fetched up on the bar years ago.

"You can hang your stuff to dry on the roots."

"I don't like that spot."

"What can I say? This was the best looking bar this late in the day."

"What about over there?"

Charley pointed across the gravel bar, away from the beach where

our rafts rested. I'd looked over there. That was the first thing I'd done after hitting the beach. Sometimes the inside of a big gravel bar is the best
place to camp. Spring floods leave fine gravel and sand in higher spots away
from main channels, and those spots are often more sheltered from the wind
by willow or alder thickets. Across the bar, a stream emerged from a copse
of cottonwood, spawning a necklace of clear pools leading into a slough. A
black gravel and sand beach big enough for two or three tents faced the highest pool, where a dozen reddening sockeye swam in a gyre. The water was so
clear and unruffled you could see every subtle twitch of their tails. I thought
camping there was akin to camping on a bear trail. But, I didn't want to say
that.

"It's a long way from the kitchen," I said. "You'd have to walk around
that tangle of uprooted trees."

"Have you seen the beach?"

"Sure. It seemed pretty beary to me."

"I didn't see any tracks."

"That doesn't mean one won't show up. The sockeyes could've just
gotten there."

"If there aren't any tracks, I'm not too worried."

"Okay."

Charley shouldered his blue dry bag and carried it across the bar to
the opposite beach. Our sky blue 14-foot raft rested on a gravel patch in front
of the kitchen. Next to it sat a darker blue 14-foot raft and a small green
cataraft. The tents of old friends Big Jim and Jack and the two Johns were
crowded into a gravel spot close to the Nushagak River's edge. Matt had
busted off thick limbs from a spruce log and started a fire. He had a fork in
one hand and knelt next to a grill with reindeer sausage roasting over orange
and grey coals. He saw Charley walking across the bar and stood up.

"He's pitching his tent over there?"

"Looks like it. What about you?"

Matt was twenty, almost as tall as Charley, and wore his West High
cross-country ski jacket, which still fit him although a little short in the

sleeves. Buff from a summer crewing on a salmon seiner in Southeast Alaska called the *Marshall Tito*, his blond hair crept out from under a green and grey baseball cap from *Ocean Beauty*, the processor that bought their fish. He twisted his lips.

"Nah. It seems like a long way from the kitchen. Do you know what's going on with Charley?"

"I don't."

I said I wanted to go for a walk and left Matt with the fire. I needed to sort things out. A Steinbeck character once said a man needs a "spot in which to wonder about things." That character grew up in a New England sea town, and his spot was a little cave in a stone bulwark on an old wharf where he could sit cross-legged. I grew up on the rivers of Interior Alaska. My spot is a long gravel bar during the height of summer, where I can wander about different benches and beaches with a captivating disarray of rocks and driftwood and feathers and bleaching bones and plants living on the fringe. It is along such a bar I can clear my head.

I walked upriver, picking up rocks here and there, looking at their wet bottoms to see the true colors. Clouds shifting from grey to black to grey had dominated the way downriver from our last camp, but yellow rays of an August sun started to shine down. Charley and Matt may have been cut from the same mold but were different sorts on the day they were born. When I held Charley in both hands for the first time, he would only open his eyes when he thought I wasn't looking, and snapped them shut whenever I looked down. The first time I held Matt to my chest I sat next to Beth on the edge of the hospital bed. He grabbed my shirt in his hands and climbed over my shoulder so fast I didn't catch him until I reached behind as he fell down my back.

Was it still that way? No matter. They both had to put up with their parent's dreams. When my grandmother first met the boys, I told her I wanted them to cross-country ski during long Alaska winters and be wilderness travelers during summers. Beth added that she wanted them to have music in their lives every day.

"A busy boy is a good boy," grandma said.

We kept them busy, and took them on as many wilderness adventures as we could. Charley was full of curiosity and very talkative in the outdoors. He was also sensitive, cringing and turning his head every time he bashed a fish with a rock. Matt was always behind his brother in years, of course, but his enthusiasm made up for it. When Matt was six, he was the first of the two to build a fire. He watched me carve shavings from an only partially dry piece of willow with my Swiss Army knife, and light them with a burning strip of duct tape. Twenty minutes later he sat on his heels with a broad smile in front of a willow fire just bursting into flame. Charley jumped into action then, and had his own fire burning within minutes.

The more trips they went on the more skilled they became, and they both were very good fishermen. The one constant in all the different river trips we went on was that both boys were more than just happy and gregarious on the river. They were captivated, often spending hours just watching something they thought wondrous, like a caribou hanging around camp, or bumble bees swarming around the sticky leaves of a weeping willow bush. But, when Charley was fifteen, he quit cross-country skiing, quit playing the piano, and changed his name to Chuck. That summer he went one last time with the family on a long river trip in Western Alaska. My enduring memory of that trip is of Charley renamed Chuck staring at the edge of a pool while holding his fly rod at an odd angle.

I walked up to a pile of silt deposited during the spring flood on a rocky shelf. Out of it sprouted dwarf fireweed blooming so radiantly the word magenta didn't seem adequate. I took a photo and sat next to the flowers and listened to the river. Charley was an artist at heart. In high school he won a statewide award for the most courageous piece of art, a twirling helix made from willow limbs and dried animal gut affixed to a driftwood log he had found. On the dried gut he penned a poem of yearning in black ink. At some point he decided his goal was to become an astronaut. When I said I saw him as more of an artist than a scientist, he didn't want to hear it. He chose a college with a big telescope, but dropped out after two quarters. When he returned to Anchorage, he lived with some high school buddies in a small apartment building surrounded by used car lots. They built powerful computers and worked minimum wage jobs that didn't start until the afternoon so they could game all night. Beth and I were in despair and I didn't know what to do. Was it a lack of confidence? Should I insist he get his act together?

When Matt told us Charley had thrown his computer out the second floor window of the apartment, Beth and I decided to act. We had been planning a trip down the Colorado River through the Grand Canyon. It was scheduled to depart in late October, sixteen days in dories from Lee's Ferry to the takeout at Diamond Creek, with lots of time for hiking. We expanded our party to four and invited Charley, who anticipated being promoted from busser to server at a local restaurant.

"I've got to work," he said.

"We will reimburse you for lost wages while you're gone," I replied.

Two male friends eventually convinced him to go. We shoved off on a cloudy day and were drenched with rain at our first camp. The next day a flash flood tore through the middle of the tents. Over the next two weeks, Charley and Matt bonded with the river guides and the younger men on the trip, hiked their brains out, and were gregarious around the evening campfires. I thought I was seeing the reemergence of the Charley I had known before.

When we returned from the Colorado, he got moving. We went on a nationwide search and he ended up at Hampshire College in Massachusetts, where he focused on creative writing. Matt came back from the Colorado with a fierce determination to become more of an outdoorsman. That summer he enrolled in a National Outdoor Leadership School backpacking program in the Yukon Territory, and after his senior year he went to Argentina and Chile for a gap year with NOLS climbing, backpacking, and kayaking. When he returned, he took charge of his life, enrolled in Bates College in Maine, and worked summers on the *Marshall Tito*. We never worried about him again.

For Charley, it worked out differently. When he returned from his first year at Hampshire, he was giddy and on fire about poetry. Slam poetry. He got a job as a server in a café in midtown Anchorage, and I was relieved when he went back to Hampshire with money in his pocket. Beth and I visited him in Boston during the Thanksgiving break. He asked us to meet him in a bar off Harvard Square. Down basement steps stood a doorman taking names for an open mic, and inside was a stage and seating for a hundred. We took our seats. Poems of all sorts were read, including a sonnet in rap cadence by a young woman who had driven all the way from Florida. The slam poets started and Charley stood up.

"Well, my parents are here tonight, so you won't be hearing my usual stuff."

The crowd tittered. Charley then read a poem about coming out of Beth's womb as told through the eyes of his ten-year-old sister Natalie who was present at his birth. The crowd gave him an ovation. Beth brushed back tears. I thought he was on his way.

Charley seemed preoccupied when I visited him in the spring, and he didn't come home that summer. Instead, he moved to Boston to live in a house with half a dozen other slam poets preparing for the National Poetry Slam. He said he'd gotten two jobs, one working as a doorman in a Boston bar, and the other a server job in a café. In one of our long distance conversations there was something that set me to wondering from the way he answered "OK" when I asked him how it was going. Was he slipping? Was it depression? I didn't know. I talked it over with Beth and in July I called.

"What do you think about coming to Alaska in August for a river trip?"

"I'd like that, dad, but the poetry slam is in August in Florida."

"You'll have enough time. I'll pay for the ticket."

He said he could get the time off from his job as doorman, and it didn't matter with the café job anyway. I didn't know then what I know now. All I knew was that he had seemed captivated on many river trips growing up, and the Colorado had done him some good.

A mother merganser brought me back when it sped away from a low bank. Ocher head feathers gave her the appearance of having a rusty butch cut. Eight little mergansers rocked back and forth in line behind her, trying to keep up. The Nushagak River in Western Alaska had been part of my life for twenty years. It's nearly three hundred miles long from its headwaters in the Alaska Range to Bristol Bay, and over those years I had paddled most its length and many of its tributaries. The family had floated the Upper Nushagak before, so we all knew what to expect. A long ride north from Dillingham in a Tikchik Airventures Beaver to the Big Bend of the Nushagak, and then south through forested hills down a clear river loaded with gravel bars, riffles, and cohos, rainbows, Dolly Varden, and arctic char. My old river running buddies Jack and Big Jim and two others named John decided to go along. They'd all known Charley and Matt since they were infants. I hoped the Upper Nushagak would do the same as the Colorado for Charley.

But, it wasn't the same. From the first day Charley was withdrawn and hung around the edge of conversations. He watched silently in the raft, fished listlessly, and retreated to his tent after meals. The only time I heard him animated is when we stopped the rafts to climb a hill off the river. Charley and Matt were in front as we crossed a broad tundra meadow full of tussocks. My left hip was in rough shape and I fell behind, but I could hear Charley talking in front of me, telling the story of an idea he had for a science fiction novel where a colonized moon became a military power and waged war on the Earth. When I caught up with them at the top, Charley sat on his haunches while the others stood to get the better view of the river winding through spruce covered hills. On the way back down to the raft I kept telling myself "he's an adult." What could I do?

When the sky suddenly darkened, I realized I'd wondered long enough about my oldest son and it was time to go back. The reindeer sausages were off the grill and another cooking fire was burning when I walked up. It was the other raft's turn to cook dinner and their plan was for roast rack of lamb. Everyone stood around the fire, drinks in hand. Flames reflected off wet rocks. I glimpsed something moving out of the corner of my eye and looked toward the beach where Charley had pitched his blue tent. A brown bear frisked behind it. From my vantage point, it looked like the bear was about to frisk right into his tent. I pretended I hadn't seen and looked in the opposite direction. After a few heart beats Big Jim spoke.

"Charley."

He pointed toward the tent and the bear. Charley slipped away from the conversation and started walking around the bar. Matt followed and said he would help. A few minutes later the boys tiptoed away from the beach toward our side of the river, Matt carrying the tent upside down while Charley carried his dry bag. Big Jim stood on our side taking photos with a telephoto lens. I didn't say a word.

The next day was our last. Our rafts played tag, passing each other while looking for the best pools, but coho salmon were only trickling through, the fishing for rainbows had been spotty, and I hadn't even seen an arctic char. Matt pulled our raft over into a place where he and I could hop out and take a leak. When we returned, Charley's fishing rod was bent over and the red stripe of a rainbow streaked back and forth in a pool I hadn't even noticed. Charley had hooked into the biggest rainbow trout of the trip. When it surged, Charley kept his tip up and feathered the drag on his fly reel with three fingers on his right hand. Then he reeled in, keeping the line tight. The rainbow surged again. Charley brought it back again. When the fish started to tire, he talked to it.

"Come to daddy."

He gently pulled it into the shallows and kept its gills underwater while removing the fly. He looked up with a satisfied smile. I thought he was connecting.

Had he felt the pulse of the wilderness again?

Could I ever hope to reel him back in?

ON THE WAY TO GAAMAAK COVE

Beth steadied her pose, left leg bent at the knee, left arm stretched ahead, right arm back. She wore blue river shorts and a sleeveless white synthetic t-shirt, and she'd tucked an eagle feather in her hair. It was high tide and the mouth of Jackpot Creek swirled slowly behind her, reflecting green spruce and darker green hemlock reaching up to snow covered mountains. The sky was blue and the air was warm and pregnant with the aroma of seawater and rotting eelgrass. Our loaded sea kayaks rocked on a sandy beach, but I focused on Beth. I never tired of watching.

Beth had a tricky back from years of bending over and picking salmon from gillnets. Stretching and yoga were the remedies, and stopping during the day for such therapy was a necessary part of many river and ocean trips. We thought we might as well choose nice spots for her to unroll a foam pad, and I always savored my role of tending the boats and watching. Once, on a sandy beach inside a rocky point, I watched Beth thrust her right knee forward and hold her palms high in a warrior pose while a humpback whale slapped the water behind her with a giant pectoral fin.

A water taxi had dropped us off in western Prince William Sound. Our plan was to paddle southwest through a waterway called Dangerous Passage to Gaamaak Cove at the head of Icy Bay. From there we could portage over an isthmus to Nassau Fjord and paddle to the tidewater face of Chenega Glacier. Beth pinged her back while assembling her collapsible kayak. We found a small island with a grassy spot she could stretch on, and a beach log where we could set up our kitchen. In all directions it was black water, green islands, and snow capped mountains. The only sounds were waves lapping on rocks.

Over the next few days we made short moves, stopping often for therapeutic reasons. On a sunny afternoon, we vacated a pocket beach and paddled into Jackpot Bay on an incoming tide. At the head of the bay we found Jackpot Creek tucked behind a rocky knoll overlooking two sandy beaches. The rising tide in the mouth of the creek created a bathing pool surrounded by tall grass. We stripped down and strode in. Beth bent over and cupped her hair in her hands. I scrubbed her back using my bandanna, something I'd done many times before. Her breasts wobbled in the reflecting pool below while I lingered above along the curve of her hips. Later, we lay entwined on a foam pad while the heads of seals bobbed in the pool.

The next morning the tide was set to ebb and it was fifteen miles to Gaamaak Cove. Beth finished her pose, took the eagle feather out of her hair, stuffed her yoga pad in her kayak, and we launched. Once out of the bay the coastline turned rugged and a rising wind blew in our faces. We pulled into a quiet spot behind Icy Point to wait and see if the wind would subside. Whitecaps riding on top of blue green waves pushed blue and white icebergs past. Inside the point was a crescent of yellow sand tucked along a rock wall. The sand and wall were out of the wind and felt hot in the sun. Beth peeled off her paddling jacket and pants. She sat on her heels, chin up, shoulder blades rolled back, elbows curled behind her. Then she pulled off her river shorts and long underwear and started another chest opener, breasts thrust toward the sun. I moved behind her. Sweat trickled down the back of her neck. I licked it and it tasted like salt. I wondered what would happen if a pleasure boat came by, but peeled down anyway. Beth turned, her moon shaped face in a shy smile. We stayed for two hours.

Three more times we stopped to wait, beaching in small bights, climbing hillsides to sit in berry patches and watch hummingbirds, all while wind and waves and icebergs sailed by. At ten in the evening we arrived at Arbor Point, the true entrance to Icy Bay, where steep basalt cliffs plunged down along boulders stacked up at the bottom. Some boulders were half in the sea with surge from breaking waves swirling around them. I tucked the bow of my kayak into a space between two while surge lifted me high enough to peek ahead. All I could see were waves breaking. I backed the kayak out.

"Maybe we should turn back and make camp."

Beth studied my face. Over the years I'd learned she had a better stomach for big seas than I did.

"We didn't come this far to leave without seeing the glaciers," she said.

We leaned toward each other as surge rocked the kayaks, and concocted a plan to paddle ahead into the wind while trying to angle closer to the rocky shore we knew was beyond the point. When we paddled out from behind the boulders and could actually see ahead, I thought it was a mistake, but it was too late to turn around. The point curled around in a long, steep face toward a distant rocky shore. Waves broke over boulders and slapped into the wall clear out of sight. If we kept our bows into the wind, we would soon be a half-mile offshore. If we moved directly toward the shore, we would be fighting waves pummeling us from the port side. I held my bow into the wind on big waves and quartered toward shore on smaller ones, using my paddle to brace while a wave broke over my bow and splashed me in the face. I looked over my shoulder. Beth was behind me, her orange paddling jacket standing out in the churning teal-colored sea.

"DOUG, STAY CLOSE," she shouted.

Her kayak plunged down the back of a wave, bow burying in the trough and then bobbing to the surface, water running off the deck. I held steady with my bow into the wind until she was off my starboard side. We both inched forward, steadying during the big waves and quartering during the smaller ones. Arbor Point faded behind us, but when I glanced back, I spotted a stretch of sand between two cliffs. I wanted to turn, to embrace the beach, but I knew it was too early. I waved at Beth and pointed ahead.

"LET'S GO UNTIL WE CAN RUN DOWNWIND."

We knew we would eventually be able to turn toward the beach with the wind on our backs. Then it would be a fast paddle to the sand. Beth waved to let me know she understood. We paddled ahead, glancing over our shoulders for what seemed like a long time. During a lull in the bigger waves, we swung our bows and turned a hundred and eighty degrees. Spray blew off the paddle before me and the kayak picked up speed. We closed fast, the bluffs on each side of the beach getting taller and taller in our eyes. I can still see details of the beach, rye grass above small waves breaking along sand. A black bear stepped out of the brush and stood along the kelp line. The area between the bluffs suddenly looked small. Then another black bear stepped out.

Juvenile delinquents.

I looked at Beth. Waves rolled away from her bow.

"NO BEARS."

She nodded and we turned back into the wind. Fifteen minutes later, I spotted a small patch of quiet water behind a cottage-sized boulder along the shore. I pointed to it and Beth waved. We paddled ahead for another ten minutes until we pivoted again to run down wind. The quiet water looked like an eddy in a river. I leaned toward it and planted my paddle to draw the bow into a rocky beach just big enough for two. Beth carved a turn with her kayak behind me. We tied the kayaks to a rock and took a walk to stretch. Above the kelp line was a sandy spot with green ryegrass, red columbine, and purple monkshood. A pair of orange-beaked oystercatchers scolded us. We found a small stream rushing out of the forest, and retrieved our water bottles. Rocky bluffs toward Gaamaak Cove towered in the gathering gloom. It was dusk, but it was midsummer, and we knew the light would stretch out. We waited until midnight, when a full moon rose above ice-covered mountains ahead of us. Weariness lines crept away from the corners of Beth's mouth.

"We can make it to the cove," I said.

She nodded, her lips half smiling. I helped her up, and we strode together to the kayaks. The longer we paddled, the higher the moon rose, and the quieter the sea became. The moon was like a headlight shining in our eyes, and all we could make out were tree skeletons and moon shadows on a long tree-covered peninsula. Loud booms echoed from Chenega Glacier calving into Nassau Fjord. Each time it boomed, hundreds of kittiwakes leaped from a cliff-top colony in the moon shadow, fluttered and flapped about in the moonlight like large bats, screeching a racket, and then settled down again on the cliff.

We paddled along a rocky beach with tiny waves lapping against it. The isthmus between Gaamaak Cove and Nassau Fjord had turned into a spit at high tide, and a current carried us across the bar to a bright moonlit beach. We dragged the kayaks up into some rye grass and walked through it to a flat spot of beach gravel, where we pitched our tent with a view both directions. Beth crawled in to zip our sleeping bags together while I walked back. The moon's reflection across black water had caught my attention. At the beach, a bright line started at my feet and continued to the far side of the cove. I gazed at it from one end to the other. In the middle, the silvery line broke into splinters and shimmered where the current from the flood swirled and dimpled the surface. Beyond the turbulence it cleared again into an unwavering line until disappearing at the edge of a black forest. I thought of Jackpot Creek and Icy Point and how far we'd come. The glacier boomed. Kittiwakes screeched and flapped and fluttered. Beth unzipped the tent door and called for me to come in.

ACKNOWLEDGMENTS

This book would never have come into existence without the encouragement, input, and honest criticism of James P. Sweeney, Bill Sherwonit, Patt Garrett, Deb Liggett, Mike Burwell, Tonja Woelber, Buffy McKay, Sherry Simpson, Rich Chiappone, J. P. O'Grady, Dan Branch, Nancy Lord, David Stevenson, John Straley, Frank Soos, Beth Pope, Patrice Parker, Martha Amore, Sandy Kleven, Seth Kantner, and Jonathon Evison. Thanks to all, and write-on.

Beth Pope, John Sund, and Ron Biggers contributed photos.

Cirque, A Literary Journal of the Pacific North Rim, previously published "Kennicott Crossing," "Arctic Char," and "Falling."

I'm grateful to the *Anchorage Daily News* and Craig Medred for providing me a fifteen-year platform for stories and photos in the Sunday "Outdoors" section. Those stories contained early seeds of "Tikchik Delta," "Showdown At Nimgun Creek," "The Congressman," and "Toe Story."

ABOUT THE AUTHOR

Doug Pope was born and raised in Interior Alaska. When he was twelve, after spending a winter night on a bed of spruce boughs in an army surplus sleeping bag, he read Jack London's *To Build A Fire*. His first non-fiction story, published when he was in high school, was set in a drafty trapper's shelter while four friends struggled to feed a fire at forty-five below. His writings have appeared in *Alpinist*, *American Alpine Journal*, *Alaska Dispatch*, *Cirque*, *A Literary Journal of the Pacific North Rim*, and the *Fairbanks Daily News-Miner*, and his writings and photos have appeared in the *Anchorage Daily News* and the *Anchorage Press*.

He lives in Hope, Alaska with his wife Beth.

ABOUT THE ARTIST

Angela Ramirez is an artist and former Denali National Park ranger. She lives in Spenard, Alaska, where she rides her bike all winter and vigorously defends her artistic vision.

ABOUT CIRQUE PRESS

Cirque Press grew out of *Cirque*, a literary journal established in 2009 by Michael Burwell, as a vehicle for the publication of writers and artists of the North Pacific Rim. This region is broadly defined as reaching north from Oregon to the Yukon Territory and south through Alaska to Hawaii – and west to the Russian Far East. Sandra Kleven joined *Cirque* in 2012 working as a partner with Burwell.

Our contributors are widely published in an array of journals. Their writing is significant. It is personal. It is strong. It draws on these regions in ways that add to the culture of places.

We felt that the works of individual writers could be lost if it were to remain scattered across the literary landscape. Therefore, we established a press to collect these writing efforts. Cirque Press seeks to gather the work of our contributors into book form where it can be experienced coherently as statement, observation, and artistry.

Sandra Kleven – Michael Burwell, publishers and editors
www.cirquejournal.com

BOOKS BY CIRQUE PRESS

Apportioning the Light by Karen Tschannen (2018)

The Lure of Impermanence by Carey Taylor (2018)

Echolocation by Kristin Berger (2018)

Like Painted Kites & Collected Works by Clifton Bates (2019)

Athabaskan Fractal: Poems of the Far North by Karla Linn Merrifield (2019)

Holy Ghost Town by Tim Sherry (2019)

Drunk on Love: Twelve Stories to Savor Responsibly by Kerry Dean Feldman (2019)

Wide Open Eyes: Surfacing from Vietnam by Paul Kirk Haeder (2020)

Silty Water People by Vivian Faith Prescott (2020)

Life Revised by Leah Stenson (2020)

Oasis Earth: Planet in Peril by Rick Steiner (2020)

The Way to Gaamaak Cove by Doug Pope

Loggers Don't Make Love by Dave Rowan

The Dream That Is Childhood by Sandra Wassilie

Seward Soundboard by Sean Ulman

FURTHER PRAISE FOR ON THE WAY TO GAAMAAK COVE

With imagery by turns terrifying and heart warming, *The Way to Gaamaak Cove* carries you through the mountains and bouldered tidewater passages of an Alaskan life in all its luminous complexities. Doug Pope knows that sometimes the most satisfying journey is a step from under a rain-pummeled tarp and into the zipped-together sleeping bags where your lover awaits you, warm and dry and already planning the next adventure.

> **Richard Chiappone**, author of *Liar's Code: Growing Up Fishing*, and *Water of an Undetermined Depth*

Doug Pope's *The Way to Gaamaak Cove* is not only a beautifully written collection of adventure essays, it is also a meditative reflection on marriage, family, and the meaning of life. In the book, Pope asks himself: 'Is love your greatest risk or is risk your greatest love?' Through his thrilling adventures through Alaska's spectacular landscape, Pope explores the dicey terrain of love and risk.

> **Martha Amore**, author of *In The Quiet Season and Other Stories*

The Way to Gaamaak Cove is Doug Pope's love letter to the great wild rivers of Alaska: the Andreafsky, the Noatak, the Gulkana, the Upper Nushagak, among others. It's also a love letter to arctic char, bears, rain, and most of all: the people he holds dearest. It's a beautiful ride: grab a paddle and dip in.

> **David Stevenson**, author of *Letters From Chamonix*, *Forty Crows*, and *Warnings Against Myself: Meditations on a Life in Climbing*

Made in the USA
Columbia, SC
30 September 2020